Effective Akka

Jamie Allen

Beijing · Cambridge · Farnham · Köln · Sebastopol · Tokyo

Effective Akka

by Jamie Allen

Printed in the United States of America.

Published by O'Reilly Media, Inc., 1005 Gravenstein Highway North, Sebastopol, CA 95472.

O'Reilly books may be purchased for educational, business, or sales promotional use. Online editions are also available for most titles (*http://my.safaribooksonline.com*). For more information, contact our corporate/institutional sales department: 800-998-9938 or *corporate@oreilly.com*.

Editor: Meghan Blanchette	**Cover Designer:** Randy Comer
Production Editor: Kara Ebrahim	**Interior Designer:** David Futato
Proofreader: Amanda Kersey	**Illustrator:** Rebecca Demarest

August 2013:   First Edition

Revision History for the First Edition:

2013-08-15:   First release

See *http://oreilly.com/catalog/errata.csp?isbn=9781449360078* for release details.

ISBN: 978-1-449-36007-8

[LSI]

Table of Contents

Preface. v

1. Actor Application Types. 1
Domain-driven   1
    Domain-driven Messages Are "Facts"   2
Work Distribution   2
    Routers and Routees   3
    BalancingDispatcher Will Be Deprecated Soon!   7
    Work Distribution Messages Are "Commands"   8

2. Patterns of Actor Usage. 9
The Extra Pattern   9
    The Problem   9
    Avoiding Ask   11
    Capturing Context   12
    Sending Yourself a Timeout Message   14
The Cameo Pattern   20
    The Companion Object Factory Method   23
    How to Test This Logic   23

3. Best Practices. 25
Actors Should Do Only One Thing   25
    Single Responsibility Principle   25
    Create Specific Supervisors   26
    Keep the Error Kernel Simple   28
    Failure Zones   29
Avoid Blocking   31
    Futures Delegation Example   32
    Pre-defining Parallel Futures   34

Parallel Futures with the zip() Method 35
Sequential Futures 35
Callbacks versus Monadic Handling 36
Futures and ExecutionContext 36
Push, Don't Pull 37
When You Must Block 39
Managed Blocking in Scala 39
Avoid Premature Optimization 40
Start Simple 40
Layer in Complexity via Indeterminism 42
Optimize with Mutability 42
Prepare for Race Conditions 44
Be Explicit 46
Name Actors and ActorSystem Instances 46
Create Specialized Messages 46
Create Specialized Exceptions 47
Beware the "Thundering Herd" 48
Don't Expose Actors 49
Avoid Using this 49
The Companion Object Factory Method 50
Never Use Direct References 52
Don't Close Over Variables 52
Use Immutable Messages with Immutable Data 54
Help Yourself in Production 54
Make Debugging Easier 55
Add Metrics 55
Externalize Business Logic 55
Use Semantically Useful Logging 56
Aggregate Your Logs with a Tool Like Flume 57
Use Unique IDs for Messages 58
Tune Akka Applications with the Typesafe Console 58
Fixing Starvation 58
Sizing Dispatchers 60
The Parallelism-Factor Setting 60
Actor Mailbox Size 60
Throughput Setting 61
Edge Cases 61

Preface

Welcome to *Effective Akka*. In this book, I will provide you with comprehensive information about what I've learned using the Akka toolkit to solve problems for clients in multiple industries and use cases. This is a chronicle of patterns I've encountered, as well as best practices for developing applications with the Akka toolkit.

Who This Book Is For

This book is for developers who have progressed beyond the introductory stage of writing Akka applications and are looking to understand best practices for development that will help them avoid common missteps. Many of the tips are relevant outside of Akka as well, whether it is using another actor library, Erlang, or just plain asynchronous development. This book is not for developers who are new to Akka and are looking for introductory information.

What Problems Are We Solving with Akka?

The first question that has to be addressed is, what problems is Akka trying to solve for application developers? Primarily, Akka provides a programming model for building distributed, asynchronous, high-performance software. Let's investigate each of these individually.

Distributed

Building applications that can scale outward, and by that I mean across multiple JVMs *and* physical machines, is very difficult. The most critical aspects a developer must keep in mind are resilience and replication: create multiple instances of similar classes for handling failure, but in a way that also performs within the boundaries of your application's nonfunctional requirements. Note that while these aspects are important in enabling developers to deal with failures in distributed systems, there are other important aspects, such as partitioning functionality, that are not specific to failure. There is a latency overhead associated with applications that are distributed across machines and/or JVMs due to network traffic as communication takes place between systems. This is particularly true if they are stateful and require synchronization across nodes, as messages must be serialized/marshalled, sent, received, and deserialized/unmarshalled for every message.

In building our distributed systems, we want to have multiple servers capable of handling requests from clients in case any one of them is unavailable for any reason. But we also do not want to have to write code throughout our application focused only on the details of sending and receiving remote messages. We want our code to be declarative —not full of details about *how* an operation is to be done, but explaining *what* is to be done. Akka gives us that ability by making the location of actors transparent across nodes.

Asynchronous

Asynchrony can have benefits both within a single machine and across a distributed architecture. In a single node, it is entirely possible to have tremendous throughput by organizing logic to be synchronous and pipelined. The Disruptor Pattern by LMAX (*http://lmax-exchange.github.io/disruptor/*) is an excellent example of an architecture that can handle a great deal of events in a single-threaded model. That said, it meets a very specific use case profile: high volume, low latency, and the ability to structure consumption of a queue. If data is not coming into the producer, the disruptor must find ways to keep the thread of execution busy so as not to lose the warmed caches that make it so efficient. It also uses pre-allocated, mutable states to avoid garbage collection —very efficient, but dangerous if developers don't know what they're doing.

With asynchronous programming, we are attempting to solve the problem of not pinning threads of execution to a particular core, but instead allowing all threads access in a varying model of fairness. We want to provide a way for the hardware to be able to utilize cores to the fullest by staging work for execution. This can lead to a lot of context switches, as different threads are scheduled to do their work on cores, which aren't friendly to performance, since data must be loaded into the on-core caches of the CPU when that thread uses it. So you also need to be able to provide ways to batch asynchronous execution. This makes the implementation less fair but allows the developer to tune threads to be more cache-friendly.

High Performance

This is one of those loose terms that, without context, might not mean much. For the sake of this book, I want to define high performance as the ability to handle tremendous loads very fast while at the same time being fault tolerant. Building a distributed system that is extremely fast but incapable of managing failure is virtually useless: failures happen, particularly in a distributed context (network partitions, node failures, etc.), and resilient systems are able deal with them. But no one wants to create a resilient system without being able to support reasonably fast execution.

Reactive Applications

You may have heard discussion, particularly around Typesafe, of creating *reactive* applications. My initial response to this word was to be cynical, having heard plenty of "marketecture" terms (words with no real architectural meaning for application development but used by marketing groups). However, the concepts espoused in the Reactive Manifesto (*http://reactivemanifesto.org*) make a strong case for what features comprise a reactive application and what needs to be done to meet this model. Reactive applications are characteristically interactive, fault tolerant, scalable, and event driven. If any of these four elements are removed, it's easy to see the impact on the other three.

Akka is one of the toolkits through which you can build reactive applications. Actors are event driven by nature, as communication can only take place through messages. Akka also provides a mechanism for fault tolerance through actor supervision, and is scalable by leveraging not only all of the cores of the machine on which it's deployed, but also by allowing applications to scale outward by using clustering and remoting to deploy the application across multiple machines or VMs.

Use Case for This Book: Banking Service for Account Data

In this book, we will use an example of a large financial institution that has decided that using existing caching strategies no longer meet the real-time needs of its business. We will break down the data as customers of the bank, who can have multiple accounts. These accounts need to be organized by type, such as checking, savings, brokerage, etc., and a customer can have multiple accounts of each type.

Conventions Used in This Book

The following typographical conventions are used in this book:

Italic
    Indicates new terms, URLs, email addresses, filenames, and file extensions.

`Constant width`
    Used for program listings, as well as within paragraphs to refer to program elements such as variable or function names, databases, data types, environment variables, statements, and keywords.

`Constant width bold`
    Shows commands or other text that should be typed literally by the user.

Constant width italic

Shows text that should be replaced with user-supplied values or by values determined by context.

This icon signifies a tip, suggestion, or general note.

This icon indicates a warning or caution.

Using Code Examples

Supplemental material (code examples, exercises, etc.) is available for download at *http://examples.oreilly.com/9781449360078-files/*.

This book is here to help you get your job done. In general, if this book includes code examples, you may use the code in this book in your programs and documentation. You do not need to contact us for permission unless you're reproducing a significant portion of the code. For example, writing a program that uses several chunks of code from this book does not require permission. Selling or distributing a CD-ROM of examples from O'Reilly books does require permission. Answering a question by citing this book and quoting example code does not require permission. Incorporating a significant amount of example code from this book into your product's documentation does require permission.

We appreciate, but do not require, attribution. An attribution usually includes the title, author, publisher, and ISBN. For example: "*Effective Akka* by Jamie Allen (O'Reilly). Copyright 2013 Jamie Allen, 978-1-449-36007-8."

If you feel your use of code examples falls outside fair use or the permission given above, feel free to contact us at *permissions@oreilly.com*.

Safari® Books Online

Safari Books Online is an on-demand digital library that delivers expert content in both book and video form from the world's leading authors in technology and business.

Technology professionals, software developers, web designers, and business and creative professionals use Safari Books Online as their primary resource for research, problem solving, learning, and certification training.

Safari Books Online offers a range of product mixes and pricing programs for organizations, government agencies, and individuals. Subscribers have access to thousands of books, training videos, and prepublication manuscripts in one fully searchable database from publishers like O'Reilly Media, Prentice Hall Professional, Addison-Wesley Professional, Microsoft Press, Sams, Que, Peachpit Press, Focal Press, Cisco Press, John Wiley & Sons, Syngress, Morgan Kaufmann, IBM Redbooks, Packt, Adobe Press, FT Press, Apress, Manning, New Riders, McGraw-Hill, Jones & Bartlett, Course Technology, and dozens more. For more information about Safari Books Online, please visit us online.

How to Contact Us

Please address comments and questions concerning this book to the publisher:

O'Reilly Media, Inc.
1005 Gravenstein Highway North
Sebastopol, CA 95472
800-998-9938 (in the United States or Canada)
707-829-0515 (international or local)
707-829-0104 (fax)

We have a web page for this book, where we list errata, examples, and any additional information. You can access this page at *http://oreil.ly/effective-akka*.

To comment or ask technical questions about this book, send email to *bookquestions@oreilly.com*.

For more information about our books, courses, conferences, and news, see our website at *http://www.oreilly.com*.

Find us on Facebook: *http://facebook.com/oreilly*

Follow us on Twitter: *http://twitter.com/oreillymedia*

Watch us on YouTube: *http://www.youtube.com/oreillymedia*

Acknowledgments

Thanks to my wife, Yeon, and children Sophie, Layla, and James—I couldn't have done this without their love, help, and support. And to my parents, Jim and Toni Allen, who displayed tremendous patience with me while I figured out what I was going to do with my life. Finally, thanks to Jonas Bonér, Viktor Klang, Roland Kuhn, Dragos Manolescu, and Thomas Lockney for their help and guidance.

CHAPTER 1

Actor Application Types

One of the questions I encounter the most when speaking at conferences is, "What is a use case for an Actor-based application?" That depends on what you're trying to accomplish, but if you want to build an application that can manage concurrency, scale outwardly across nodes, and be fault tolerant, actors are a good fit for this role.

Domain-driven

In a domain-driven actor application, actors live and die to represent the state of the world in a live cache, where the mere existence of these actors and their encapsulation of state show the data for your application. They are frequently used in systems where information is provisioned to multiple other servers, which happens in an *eventual consistency* fashion. This implies that it is plausible that an actor attempting to supply another server may not be able to do so at a given point, and therefore must try until it can.

For example, imagine a large financial institution trying to keep a real-time view of all of its customers, with all of their accounts and all of the investments that customer owns via each account at a given time. This information can be created and maintained live through actor-supervisor hierarchies.

This kind of real-time domain modeling, where you are in essence creating a cache that also contains behavior, is enabled by the lightweight nature of Akka actors. Because Akka actors share resources (such as threads), each instance only takes about 400 bytes of heap space before you begin adding state for your domain. It is plausible that one server could contain the entire business domain for a large corporation represented in Akka actors.

The added benefit of using actors for this kind of domain modeling is that they also introduce fault tolerance: you have the ability to use Akka's supervision strategies to ensure high uptime for your system, as opposed to simple caches of domain objects where exceptions have to be handled at the service layer. An example can be found in Figure 1-1.

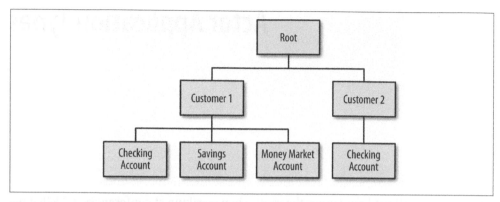

Figure 1-1. Domain-driven actors

And this truly can fit into Eric Evans' "Domain-Driven Design" paradigm. Actors can represent concepts described in the domain-driven approach, such as entities, aggregates, and aggregate roots. You can design entire context bounds with actors. When we get to the use case to show patterns, I'll show you how.

Domain-driven Messages Are "Facts"

When you build a hierarchy of domain objects represented as actors, they need to be notified about what is happening in the world around them. This is typically represented as messages passed as "facts" about an event that has occurred. While this is not a rule per se, it is a best practice to keep in mind. The domain should be responding to external events that change the world that it is modeling, and it should morph itself to meet those changes as they occur. And if something happens that prevents the domain actors from representing those changes, they should be written to eventually find consistency with them:

```
// An example of a fact message
case class AccountAddressUpdated(accountId: Long, address: AccountAddress)
```

Work Distribution

In this scenario, actors are stateless and receive messages that contain state, upon which they will perform some pre-defined action and return a new representation of some state. That is the most important differentiation between worker actors and domain actors: worker actors are meant for parallelization or separation of dangerous tasks into actors built specifically for that purpose, and the data upon which they will act is always provided to them. Domain actors, introduced in the previous section, represent a live cache where the existence of the actors and the state they encapsulate are a view of the current state of the application. There are varying strategies for how this can be implemented, each with its own benefits and use cases.

Routers and Routees

In Akka, routers are used to spawn multiple instances of one actor type so that work can be distributed among them. Each instance of the actor contains its own mailbox, and therefore this cannot be considered a "work-stealing" implementation. There are several strategies that can be used for this task, including the following sections.

Random

Random is a strategy where messages are distributed to the actors in a random fashion, which isn't one I favor. There was a recent discussion about a startup using Heroku Dynos (virtual server instances) where requests were distributed to each dyno randomly, which meant that even if users scaled up the number of dynos to handle more requests, they had no guarantee that the new endpoints would get any requests and the load would be distributed. That said, random routees are the only ones that do not incur a routing bottleneck, as nothing must be checked before the message is forwarded. And if you have a large number of messages flowing through your router, that can be a useful tradeoff.

Look at Figure 1-2. If I have five routees and use a random strategy, one routee may have no items in its mailbox (like #3), while another routee might have a bunch (#2). And the next message could also be routed to routee #2 as well.

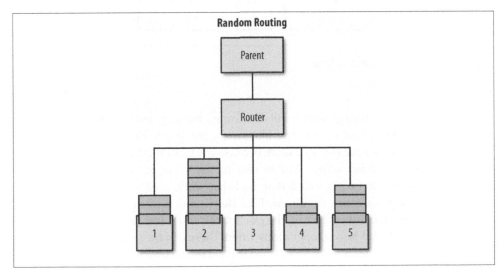

Figure 1-2. Random routing

Round robin

Round robin is a strategy where messages are distributed to each actor instance in sequence as though they were in a ring, which is good for even distribution. It spreads work sequentially amongst the routees and can be an excellent strategy when the tasks to be performed by all routees are always the same and CPU-bound. This assumes that all considerations between the routees and the boxes on which they run are equal: thread pools have threads to use for scheduling the tasks, and the machines have cores available to execute the work.

In Figure 1-3, the work has been distributed evenly, and the next message will go to routee #3.

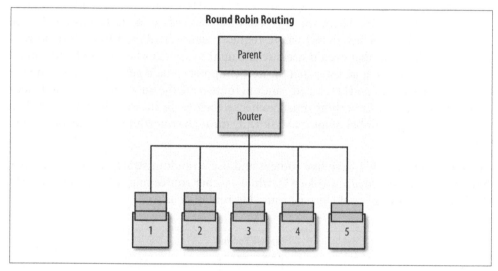

Figure 1-3. Round-robin routing

Smallest mailbox

Smallest mailbox is a strategy which will distribute a message to the actor instance with the smallest mailbox. This may sound like a panacea, but it isn't. The actor with the smallest mailbox may have the least work because the tasks it is being asked to perform take longer than the other actors'. And by placing the message into its mailbox, it may actually take longer to be processed than had that work been distributed to an actor with more messages already enqueued. Like the round-robin router, this strategy is useful for routees that always handle the exact same work, but the work is blocking in nature: for example, IO-bound operations where there can be varying latencies.

The smallest mailbox strategy does not work for remote actors. The router does not know the size of the mailbox with remote routees.

In Figure 1-4, the work will be distributed to routee #4, the actor with the least number of messages in its mailbox. This happens regardless of whether it will be received and handled faster than if it were sent to #1, which has more items but work that could take less time.

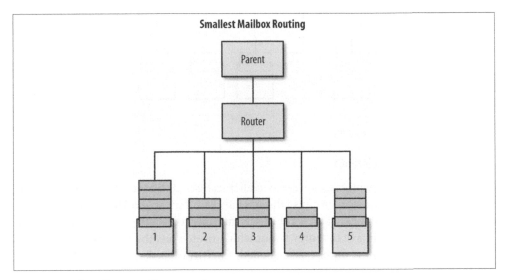

Figure 1-4. Smallest-mailbox routing

Broadcast

Broadcast is a strategy where messages are sent to all instances of the actor the router controls. It's good for distributing work to multiple nodes that may have different tasks to perform or handling fault tolerance by handing the same task to nodes that will all perform the same work, in case any failures occur.

Since all routees under the router will receive the message, their mailboxes should theoretically be equally full/empty. The reality is that how you apply the dispatcher for fairness in message handling (by tuning the "throughput" configuration value) will determine this. Try not to think of routers where the work is distributed evenly as bringing determinism to your system: it just means that work is evenly spread but could still occur in each routee at varying times. See Figure 1-5 for an example.

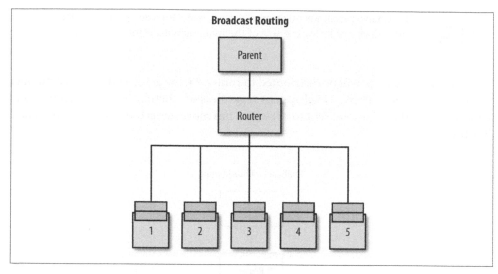

Figure 1-5. Broadcast routing

ScatterGatherFirstCompletedOf

This is a strategy where messages are sent to all instances of the actor the router controls, but only the first response from any of them is handled. This is good for situations where you need a response quickly and want to ask multiple handlers to try to do it for you. In this way, you don't have to worry about which routee has the least amount of work to do, or even if it has the fewest tasks queued, since those tasks won't take longer than another routee that already has more messages to handle.

This is particularly useful if the routees are spread among multiple JVMs or physical boxes. Each of those boxes might be utilized at varying rates, and you want the work to be performed as quickly as possible without trying to manually figure out which box is currently doing the least work. Worse, even if you did check to see if a box was the least busy, by the time you figured out which box it was and sent the work, it could be loaded down chewing through other work.

In Figure 1-6, I'm sending the work across five routees. I only care about whichever of the five completes the work first and responds. This trades some potential network latency (if the boxes are more than one physically close hop away) and extra CPU utilization (as each of the routees has to do the work) for getting the response the fastest.

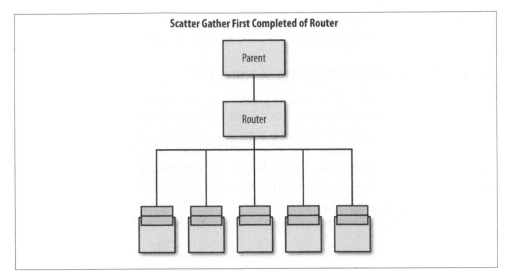

Figure 1-6. ScatterGatherFirstCompletedOf routing

Consistent hash routing

This is a new routing strategy, recently added in Akka 2.1. In some cases, you want to be certain that you understand which routee will handle specific kinds of work, possibly because you have a well-defined Akka application on several remote nodes and you want to be sure that work is sent to the closest server to avoid latency. It will also be relevant to cluster aware routing in a similar way. This is powerful because you know that, by hash, work will most likely be routed to the same routee that handled earlier versions of the same work. Consistent hashing, by definition, does not guarantee even distribution of work.

BalancingDispatcher Will Be Deprecated Soon!

I mentioned earlier that each actor in a router cannot share mailboxes, and therefore work stealing is not possible even with the varying strategies that are available. Akka used to solve this problem with the BalancingDispatcher, where all actors created with that dispatcher share *one* mailbox, and in doing so, can grab the next message when they have finished their current work. Work-stealing is an extremely powerful concept, and because the implementation required using a specific dispatcher, it also isolated the workers on their own thread pool, which is extremely important for avoiding actor starvation.

However, the BalancingDispatcher has been found to be quirky and not recommended for general usage, given its exceptional and somewhat unexpected behavior. It is going to be deprecated shortly in lieu of a new router type in an upcoming version of Akka to handle work-stealing semantics, but that is as yet undefined. The Akka team does not recommend using `BalancingDispatcher`, so stay away from it.

Work Distribution Messages Are "Commands"

When you are distributing work among actors to be performed, you typically will send commands that the actors can respond to and thus complete the task. The message includes the data required for the actor to perform the work, and you should refrain from putting state into the actor required to complete the computation. The task should be idempotent—any of the many routee instances could handle the message, and you should always get the same response given the same input, without side effects:

```
// An example of a command message
case class CalculateSumOfBalances(balances: List[BigDecimal])
```

CHAPTER 2

Patterns of Actor Usage

Now that we understand the varying types of actor systems that can be created, what are some patterns of usage that we can define so that we can avoid making common mistakes when writing actor-based applications? Let's look at a few of them.

The Extra Pattern

One of the most difficult tasks in asynchronous programming is trying to capture context so that the state of the world at the time the task was started can be accurately represented at the time the task finishes. However, creating anonymous instances of Akka actors is a very simple and lightweight solution for capturing the context at the time the message was handled to be utilized when the tasks are successfully completed. They are like extras in the cast of a movie—helping provide realistic context to the primary actors who are working around them.

The Problem

A great example is an actor that is sequentially handling messages in its mailbox but performing the tasks based on those messages off-thread with futures. This is a great way to design your actors in that they will not block waiting for responses, allowing them to handle more messages concurrently and increase your application's performance. However, the state of the actor will likely change with every message.

Let's define the boilerplate of this example. These are classes that will be reused for each of the iterations of our development process going forward. Note that all of this code is available in my GitHub repository (*https://github.com/jamie-allen/effective_akka*), should you want to clone it and test yourself. First, we have a message telling our actor to retrieve the customer account balances for a particular customer ID:

```
case class GetCustomerAccountBalances(id: Long)
```

Next, we have data transfer objects in which we return the requested account information. Because customers may or may not have any accounts of each type, and it is possible they may have more than one of any of the account types, we return `Option [List[(Long, BigDecimal)]]` in each case, where `Long` represents an account identifier, and `BigDecimal` represents a balance:

```
case class AccountBalances(
  val checking: Option[List[(Long, BigDecimal)]],
  val savings: Option[List[(Long, BigDecimal)]],
  val moneyMarket: Option[List[(Long, BigDecimal)]])
case class CheckingAccountBalances(
  val balances: Option[List[(Long, BigDecimal)]])
case class SavingsAccountBalances(
  val balances: Option[List[(Long, BigDecimal)]])
case class MoneyMarketAccountBalances(
  val balances: Option[List[(Long, BigDecimal)]])
```

I promised in the preface of this book that I would show how this ties back to Eric Evans' concepts with domain-driven design. Look at the classes I have created to perform this work. We can consider the entire `AccountService` to be a context bound, where an individual `CheckingAccount` or `SavingsAccount` is an entity. The number represented by the balance inside of one of those classes is a value. The `checkingBalances`, `savings Balances`, and `mmBalances` fields are aggregates, and the `AccountBalances` return type is an aggregate root. Finally, Vaughn Vernon in his excellent "Implementing Domain-Driven Design" (*https://vaughnvernon.co/*) points to Akka as a possible implementation for an event-driven context bound. It is also quite easy to implement *command query responsibility separation* (per Greg Young's specification) and *event sourcing* (using the open source eventsourced (*http://bit.ly/16EVCtN*) library) with Akka.

Finally, we have proxy traits that represent service interfaces. Just like with the Java best practice of exposing interfaces to services rather than the implementations of the classes, we will follow that convention here and define the service interfaces which can then be stubbed out in our tests:

```
trait SavingsAccountsProxy extends Actor
trait CheckingAccountsProxy extends Actor
trait MoneyMarketAccountsProxy extends Actor
```

Let's take an example of an actor that will act as a proxy to get a customer's account information for a financial services firm from multiple data sources. Further, let's assume that each of the subsystem proxies for savings, checking and money market account balances will optionally return a list of accounts and their balances of that kind for this customer, and we'll inject those as dependencies to the retriever class. Let's write some basic Akka actor code to perform this task:

```
import scala.concurrent.ExecutionContext
import scala.concurrent.duration._
import akka.actor._
```

```
import akka.pattern.ask
import akka.util.Timeout

class AccountBalanceRetriever(savingsAccounts: ActorRef,
                             checkingAccounts: ActorRef,
                             moneyMarketAccounts: ActorRef) extends Actor {
  implicit val timeout: Timeout = 100 milliseconds
  implicit val ec: ExecutionContext = context.dispatcher
  def receive = {
    case GetCustomerAccountBalances(id) =>
      val futSavings = savingsAccounts ? GetCustomerAccountBalances(id)
      val futChecking = checkingAccounts ? GetCustomerAccountBalances(id)
      val futMM = moneyMarketAccounts ? GetCustomerAccountBalances(id)
      val futBalances = for {
        savings <- futSavings.mapTo[Option[List[(Long, BigDecimal)]]]
        checking <- futChecking.mapTo[Option[List[(Long, BigDecimal)]]]
        mm <- futMM.mapTo[Option[List[(Long, BigDecimal)]]]
      } yield AccountBalances(savings, checking, mm)
      futBalances map (sender ! _)
  }
}
```

This code is fairly concise. The `AccountBalanceRetriever` actor receives a message to get account balances for a customer, and then it fires off three futures in parallel. The first will get the customer's savings account balance, the second will get the checking account balance, and the third will get a money market balance. Doing these tasks in parallel allows us to avoid the expensive cost of performing the retrievals sequentially. Also, note that while the futures will return `Options` of some account balances by account ID, if they return `None`, they will not short-circuit the `for` comprehension—if `None` is returned from `futSavings`, it will still continue the `for` comprehension.

However, there are a couple of things about it that are not ideal. First of all, it is using futures to ask other actors for responses, which creates a new `PromiseActorRef` for every message sent behind the scenes. This is a waste of resources. It would be better to have our `AccountBalanceRetriever` actor send messages out in a "fire and forget" fashion and collect results asynchronously into *one* actor.

Furthermore, there is a glaring race condition in this code—can you see it? We're referencing the "sender" in our map operation on the result from `futBalances`, which may not be the same `ActorRef` when the future completes, because the `AccountBalanceRe` `triever ActorRef` may now be handling another message from a different sender at that point!

Avoiding Ask

Let's focus on eliminating the need to ask for responses in our actor first. We can send the messages with the ! and collect responses into an optional list of balances by account number. But how would we go about doing that?

```scala
import scala.concurrent.ExecutionContext
import scala.concurrent.duration._
import akka.actor._

class AccountBalanceRetriever(savingsAccounts: ActorRef,
                              checkingAccounts: ActorRef,
                              moneyMarketAccounts: ActorRef) extends Actor {
  val checkingBalances,
      savingsBalances,
      mmBalances: Option[List[(Long, BigDecimal)]] = None
  var originalSender: Option[ActorRef] = None
  def receive = {
    case GetCustomerAccountBalances(id) =>
      originalSender = Some(sender)
      savingsAccounts ! GetCustomerAccountBalances(id)
      checkingAccounts ! GetCustomerAccountBalances(id)
      moneyMarketAccounts ! GetCustomerAccountBalances(id)
    case AccountBalances(cBalances, sBalances, mmBalances) =>
      (checkingBalances, savingsBalances, mmBalances) match {
        case (Some(c), Some(s), Some(m)) => originalSender.get !
          AccountBalances(checkingBalances, savingsBalances, mmBalances)
        case _ =>
      }
  }
}
```

This is better but still leaves a lot to be desired. First of all, we've created our collection of balances we've received back at the instance level, which means we can't differentiate the aggregation of responses to a single request to get account balances. Worse, we can't time out a request back to our original requestor. Finally, while we've captured the original sender as an instance variable that may or may not have a value (since there is no originalSender when the AccountBalanceRetriever starts up), we have no way of being sure that the originalSender is who we want it to be when we want to send data back!

Capturing Context

The problem is that we're attempting to take the result of the off-thread operations of retrieving data from multiple sources and return it to whomever sent us the message in the first place. However, the actor will likely have moved on to handling additional messages in its mailbox by the time these futures complete, and the state represented in the AccountBalanceRetriever actor for "sender" at that time could be a completely different actor instance. So how do we get around this?

The trick is to create an anonymous inner actor for each GetCustomerAccountBalances message that is being handled. In doing so, you can capture the state you need to have available when the futures are fulfilled. Let's see how:

```scala
import scala.concurrent.ExecutionContext
import scala.concurrent.duration._
import akka.actor._

class AccountBalanceRetriever(savingsAccounts: ActorRef,
                              checkingAccounts: ActorRef,
                              moneyMarketAccounts: ActorRef) extends Actor {
  val checkingBalances,
      savingsBalances,
      mmBalances: Option[List[(Long, BigDecimal)]] = None
  def receive = {
    case GetCustomerAccountBalances(id) => {
      context.actorOf(Props(new Actor() {
        var checkingBalances,
            savingsBalances,
            mmBalances: Option[List[(Long, BigDecimal)]] = None
        val originalSender = sender
        def receive = {
          case CheckingAccountBalances(balances) =>
            checkingBalances = balances
            isDone
          case SavingsAccountBalances(balances) =>
            savingsBalances = balances
            isDone
          case MoneyMarketAccountBalances(balances) =>
            mmBalances = balances
            isDone
        }

        def isDone =
          (checkingBalances, savingsBalances, mmBalances) match {
            case (Some(c), Some(s), Some(m)) =>
              originalSender ! AccountBalances(checkingBalances,
                                               savingsBalances,
                                               mmBalances)

              context.stop(self)
            case _ =>
          }

        savingsAccounts ! GetCustomerAccountBalances(id)
        checkingAccounts ! GetCustomerAccountBalances(id)
        moneyMarketAccounts ! GetCustomerAccountBalances(id)
      }))
    }
  }
}
```

This is much better. We've captured the state of each receive and only send it back to the originalSender when all three have values. But there are still two issues here. First, we haven't defined how we can time out on the original request for all of the balances back to whomever requested them. Secondly, our originalSender is *still* getting a wrong value—the "sender" from which it is assigned is actually the sender value of the anonymous inner actor, *not* the one that sent the original `GetCustomerAccountBalances` message!

Sending Yourself a Timeout Message

We can send ourselves a timeout message to handle our need to timeout the original request, by allowing another task to compete for the right to complete the operation with a timeout. This is a very clean way to allow the work to occur, while still enforcing timeout semantics on the request. If the data for all three of the account types is enqueued in the mailbox before the timeout message, the proper response of an `AccountBalances` type is sent back to the original sender. However, if the timeout message from the scheduled task is enqueued before any one of those three responses, a timeout is returned to the client.

Note that I am using `None` to represent only when I don't have any data returned from one of my specific account type proxies. In the case where a customer is looked up and no data is found, I'm expecting to receive a response of `Some(List())`, meaning no data was found for that customer in that account type. This way, I can semantically differentiate whether or not I've received a response and when no data was found.

For the sake of additional clarity, I am using the `LoggingReceive` block in this example. This tells Akka to automatically log the handling of each message dequeued from the mailbox. It is a best practice to give yourself as much information as possible at runtime so you can debug your actors, and it can easily be turned off in the configuration file for the application. For more information, see the Akka online documentation (*http://akka.io/docs/*).

```scala
import scala.concurrent.ExecutionContext
import scala.concurrent.duration._
import org.jamieallen.effectiveakka.common._
import akka.actor.{ Actor, ActorRef, Props, ActorLogging }
import akka.event.LoggingReceive

object AccountBalanceRetrieverFinal {
  case object AccountRetrievalTimeout
}

class AccountBalanceRetrieverFinal(savingsAccounts: ActorRef,
                                   checkingAccounts: ActorRef,
                                   moneyMarketAccounts: ActorRef)
                                       extends Actor with ActorLogging {
  import AccountBalanceRetrieverFinal._

  def receive = {
    case GetCustomerAccountBalances(id) => {
      log.debug(s"Received GetCustomerAccountBalances for ID: $id from $sender")
      val originalSender = sender
```

```scala
context.actorOf(Props(new Actor() {
  var checkingBalances,
      savingsBalances,
      mmBalances: Option[List[(Long, BigDecimal)]] = None
  def receive = LoggingReceive {
    case CheckingAccountBalances(balances) =>
      log.debug(s"Received checking account balances: $balances")
      checkingBalances = balances
      collectBalances
    case SavingsAccountBalances(balances) =>
      log.debug(s"Received savings account balances: $balances")
      savingsBalances = balances
      collectBalances
    case MoneyMarketAccountBalances(balances) =>
      log.debug(s"Received money market account balances: $balances")
      mmBalances = balances
      collectBalances
    case AccountRetrievalTimeout =>
      sendResponseAndShutdown(AccountRetrievalTimeout)
  }

  def collectBalances = (checkingBalances,
                         savingsBalances,
                         mmBalances) match {
    case (Some(c), Some(s), Some(m)) =>
      log.debug(s"Values received for all three account types")
      timeoutMessager.cancel
      sendResponseAndShutdown(AccountBalances(checkingBalances,
                                              savingsBalances,
                                              mmBalances))
    case _ =>
  }

  def sendResponseAndShutdown(response: Any) = {
    originalSender ! response
    log.debug("Stopping context capturing actor")
    context.stop(self)
  }

  savingsAccounts ! GetCustomerAccountBalances(id)
  checkingAccounts ! GetCustomerAccountBalances(id)
  moneyMarketAccounts ! GetCustomerAccountBalances(id)

  import context.dispatcher
  val timeoutMessager = context.system.scheduler.
      scheduleOnce(250 milliseconds) {
        self ! AccountRetrievalTimeout
      }
}))
}
```

```
    }
  }
```

Now we can collect our results and check to see if we received the expected values and place them into the `AccountBalances` result to return to the caller, while also cancelling the scheduled task so that it doesn't waste resources. Finally, we must remember to stop our anonymous inner actor so that we do not leak memory for every `GetCustomerAc countBalances` message we receive, regardless of whether we received all three responses or the timeout!

So why do we have to send the `AccountRetrievalTimeout` message to ourselves, into the queue of our `Extra` actor, rather than just sending it directly back to the `original Sender` in our `scheduleOnce` lambda? The scheduled task will run on another thread! If we perform work relative to cleaning up the actor on that thread, we're introducing concurrency into the actor. While we are only telling our actor to stop itself after sending the message in this example, it would be very easy to fall into the trap of closing over some state and manipulating it if you do not send a message to yourself. There are other interfaces for scheduling that might make it more apparent for some that the operation is asynchronous, such as the method call style seen here:

```
val timeoutMessager = context.system.scheduler.
    scheduleOnce(250 milliseconds, self, AccountRetrievalTimeout)
```

You have to be vigilant about this. Sometimes, it can be very easy to fall into the trap of introducing concurrency into our actors where there never should be any. If you see yourself using curly braces inside of an actor, think about what is happening inside of there and what you might be closing over.

Why not use a promise?

In an earlier version of this example, I tried to use a promise to perform this work, where either the successful result of the `AccountBalances` type was put into the future inside of the promise, or the timeout failure was used to complete it. However, this is unnecessary complexity, as we can allow the ordering inside of the `Extra` actor's queue of when messages are enqueued to perform the same basic task. But also, you cannot return a future value from a promise—they cannot be sent to an actor, which may or may not be remote. And due to the beauty of location transparency, that is an implementation detail on which your actors should never focus.

 Futures should never be passed between actors because you cannot serialize a thread.

How to test this logic

So now that we have some code that we think will work, we need to write tests to prove that it does. If you're a TDD-adherent, you're probably mortified that I didn't do that up front. I'm not dogmatic about *when* someone writes tests; I just care that the tests get written.

The first thing we have to do is define the test stubs that will be used in our tests and injected as dependencies to the retriever actor. These stubs can be very simple actors—when asked for account information of their type by a specific customer ID, each non-failure test case stub will return an optional list of balances by account ID. Data for each customer to be used in tests needs to be placed into a map to be found, and if no data is returned, we must return a value of `Some(List())` to meet our API:

```
import akka.actor.{ Actor, ActorLogging }
import akka.event.LoggingReceive

class CheckingAccountsProxyStub
extends CheckingAccountsProxy with ActorLogging {
  val accountData = Map[Long, List[(Long, BigDecimal)]](
    1L -> List((3, 15000)),
    2L -> List((6, 640000), (7, 1125000), (8, 40000)))

  def receive = LoggingReceive {
    case GetCustomerAccountBalances(id: Long) =>
      log.debug(s"Received GetCustomerAccountBalances for ID: $id")
      accountData.get(id) match {
        case Some(data) => sender ! CheckingAccountBalances(Some(data))
        case None => sender ! CheckingAccountBalances(Some(List()))
      }
  }
}

class SavingsAccountsProxyStub
    extends SavingsAccountsProxy with ActorLogging {

  val accountData = Map[Long, List[(Long, BigDecimal)]](
    1L -> (List((1, 150000), (2, 29000))),
    2L -> (List((5, 80000))))

  def receive = LoggingReceive {
    case GetCustomerAccountBalances(id: Long) =>
      log.debug(s"Received GetCustomerAccountBalances for ID: $id")
      accountData.get(id) match {
        case Some(data) => sender ! SavingsAccountBalances(Some(data))
        case None => sender ! SavingsAccountBalances(Some(List()))
      }
  }
}

class MoneyMarketAccountsProxyStub
    extends MoneyMarketAccountsProxy with ActorLogging {

  val accountData = Map[Long, List[(Long, BigDecimal)]](
    2L -> List((9, 640000), (10, 1125000), (11, 40000)))
```

```
def receive = LoggingReceive {
  case GetCustomerAccountBalances(id: Long) =>
    log.debug(s"Received GetCustomerAccountBalances for ID: $id")
    accountData.get(id) match {
      case Some(data) => sender ! MoneyMarketAccountBalances(Some(data))
      case None => sender ! MoneyMarketAccountBalances(Some(List()))
    }
  }
}
```

In the failure condition (represented by a timeout), a stub will simulate a long-running blocking database call that does not complete in time by never sending a response to the calling actor:

```
class TimingOutSavingsAccountProxyStub
extends SavingsAccountsProxy with ActorLogging {
  def receive = LoggingReceive {
    case GetCustomerAccountBalances(id: Long) =>
      log.debug(s"Forcing timeout by not responding!")
  }
}
```

The following examples show how to write a test case for the successful return of AccountBalances. Since this example uses stubbed out proxies to what would be services from which receive account information, it is trivial to inject test-only stub proxies that will cause the timeout functionality to occur.

We also want to be sure that the integrity of the context of each message handled is maintained by our retriever. To do this, we send multiple messages from different TestProbe instances one after the other, and we verify that the different values were appropriately returned to each.

Note how I use the within block to verify the timing of expected responses. This is a great way to verify that your tests are executing to meet the nonfunctional requirements of your system. Use the within block to specify either a maximum time of execution, or as we see in the failure case, that we didn't receive a response too early or too late.

Finally, we test the timeout condition by injecting a timing out stub into our retriever and making sure that the timeout response is what our test receives in response:

```
import akka.testkit.{ TestKit, TestProbe, ImplicitSender }
import akka.actor.{ Actor, ActorLogging, ActorSystem, Props }
import org.scalatest.WordSpecLike
import org.scalatest.matchers.MustMatchers
import scala.concurrent.duration._
import org.jamieallen.effectiveakka.common._
import org.jamieallen.effectiveakka.pattern.extra.AccountBalanceRetrieverFinal._

class ExtraFinalSpec extends TestKit(ActorSystem("ExtraTestAS"))
    with ImplicitSender with WordSpecLike with MustMatchers {
```

```scala
"An AccountBalanceRetriever" should {
  "return a list of account balances" in {
    val probe2 = TestProbe()
    val probe1 = TestProbe()
    val savingsAccountsProxy =
      system.actorOf(Props[SavingsAccountsProxyStub],
        "extra-success-savings")
    val checkingAccountsProxy =
      system.actorOf(Props[CheckingAccountsProxyStub],
        "extra-success-checkings")
    val moneyMarketAccountsProxy = system.actorOf(
      Props[MoneyMarketAccountsProxyStub], "extra-success-money-markets")
    val accountBalanceRetriever = system.actorOf(
      Props(new AccountBalanceRetrieverFinal(savingsAccountsProxy,
                                             checkingAccountsProxy,
                                             moneyMarketAccountsProxy)),
                                             "extra-retriever")

    within(300 milliseconds) {
      probe1.send(accountBalanceRetriever, GetCustomerAccountBalances(1L))
      val result = probe1.expectMsgType[AccountBalances]
      result must equal(AccountBalances(
          Some(List((3, 15000))),
          Some(List((1, 150000), (2, 29000))),
          Some(List())))
    }
    within(300 milliseconds) {
      probe2.send(accountBalanceRetriever, GetCustomerAccountBalances(2L))
      val result = probe2.expectMsgType[AccountBalances]
      result must equal(AccountBalances(
          Some(List((6, 640000), (7, 1125000), (8, 40000))),
          Some(List((5, 80000))),
          Some(List((9, 640000), (10, 1125000), (11, 40000)))))
    }
  }

  "return a TimeoutException when timeout is exceeded" in {
    val savingsAccountsProxy = system.actorOf(
      Props[TimingOutSavingsAccountProxyStub], "extra-timing-out-savings")
    val checkingAccountsProxy = system.actorOf(
      Props[CheckingAccountsProxyStub], "extra-timing-out-checkings")
    val moneyMarketAccountsProxy = system.actorOf(
      Props[MoneyMarketAccountsProxyStub], "extra-timing-out-money-markets")
    val accountBalanceRetriever = system.actorOf(
      Props(new AccountBalanceRetrieverFinal(savingsAccountsProxy,
                                             checkingAccountsProxy,
                                             moneyMarketAccountsProxy)),
                                             "extra-timing-out-retriever")
    val probe = TestProbe()

    within(250 milliseconds, 500 milliseconds) {
```

```
        probe.send(accountBalanceRetriever, GetCustomerAccountBalances(1L))
        probe.expectMsg(AccountRetrievalTimeout)
      }
    }
  }
}
```

Now our test checks the success case and that the failure results in expected behavior. And because the AccountRetrievalTimeout is a case object, it is a "term," not a "type," and I therefore can use the expectMsg() method instead of expectMsgType[].

 Asynchronous programming is simply not easy, even with powerful tools at our disposal. We always must think about the state we need and the context from which we get it *at the time we need it*.

The Cameo Pattern

The Extra Pattern does help in some scenarios, but it could easily be argued that it muddles your code by putting too many details in once place. It is also similar to lambdas, in that using an anonymous instance gives you less information in stack traces on the JVM, is harder to use with a debugging tool, and is easier to close over state.

The good news is that it is very easily fixed by using pre-defined types. You get information specific to the class that you created in stack traces without an obfuscated, generated name. And you can't close over external state, because there is none: you have to pass the data into the class for it to be visible.

There is a time and a place for everything, and that includes lambdas and anonymous implementations of interfaces, just like we did in the Extra Pattern. When the code is trivial, you can generally use these constructs without fear. However, learn to notice when the code in such literals is crossing a threshold of complexity that will make it harder to reason about in production when failure occurs.

Those are good reasons for pulling the type you're creating with the Extra Pattern into a pre-defined type of actor, where you create an instance of that type for every message handled. To do so, we can move the anonymous implementation of the actor trait out into its own type definition. This results in a type only used for simple interactions between actors, similar to a cameo role in the movies.

Let's pull the anonymous implementation out and bind it to a type. How would that look?

```
import scala.concurrent.ExecutionContext
import scala.concurrent.duration._
import org.jamieallen.effectiveakka.common._
import akka.actor._
```

```scala
import akka.event.LoggingReceive

object AccountBalanceResponseHandler {
  case object AccountRetrievalTimeout

  // Factory method for our actor Props
  def props(savingsAccounts: ActorRef, checkingAccounts: ActorRef,
    moneyMarketAccounts: ActorRef, originalSender: ActorRef): Props = {
    Props(new AccountBalanceResponseHandler(savingsAccounts, checkingAccounts,
      moneyMarketAccounts, originalSender))
  }
}

class AccountBalanceResponseHandler(savingsAccounts: ActorRef,
                                    checkingAccounts: ActorRef,
                                    moneyMarketAccounts: ActorRef,
                                    originalSender: ActorRef)
                                        extends Actor with ActorLogging {

  import AccountBalanceResponseHandler._
  var checkingBalances,
      savingsBalances,
      mmBalances: Option[List[(Long, BigDecimal)]] = None
  def receive = LoggingReceive {
    case CheckingAccountBalances(balances) =>
      log.debug(s"Received checking account balances: $balances")
      checkingBalances = balances
      collectBalances
    case SavingsAccountBalances(balances) =>
      log.debug(s"Received savings account balances: $balances")
      savingsBalances = balances
      collectBalances
    case MoneyMarketAccountBalances(balances) =>
      log.debug(s"Received money market account balances: $balances")
      mmBalances = balances
      collectBalances
    case AccountRetrievalTimeout =>
      log.debug("Timeout occurred")
      sendResponseAndShutdown(AccountRetrievalTimeout)
  }

  def collectBalances = (checkingBalances,
                         savingsBalances,
                         mmBalances) match {
    case (Some(c), Some(s), Some(m)) =>
      log.debug(s"Values received for all three account types")
      timeoutMessager.cancel
      sendResponseAndShutdown(AccountBalances(checkingBalances,
                                              savingsBalances,
                                              mmBalances))

    case _ =>
  }
```

```
def sendResponseAndShutdown(response: Any) = {
  originalSender ! response
  log.debug("Stopping context capturing actor")
  context.stop(self)
}

import context.dispatcher
val timeoutMessager = context.system.scheduler.
  scheduleOnce(250 milliseconds) {
    self ! AccountRetrievalTimeout
  }
}

class AccountBalanceRetriever(savingsAccounts: ActorRef,
                             checkingAccounts: ActorRef,
                             moneyMarketAccounts: ActorRef) extends Actor {
  def receive = {
    case GetCustomerAccountBalances(id) =>
      val originalSender = Some(sender)

      // I'm now using a factory method now from the companion object above!
      val handler = context.actorOf(
        AccountBalanceResponseHandler.props(savingsAccounts,
                            checkingAccounts,
                            moneyMarketAccounts,
                            originalSender), "cameo-message-handler")
      savingsAccounts.tell(GetCustomerAccountBalances(id), handler)
      checkingAccounts.tell(GetCustomerAccountBalances(id), handler)
      moneyMarketAccounts.tell(GetCustomerAccountBalances(id), handler)
  }
}
```

Note that now we have to use the `tell` method on the `ActorRef`s for the accounts so that we can pass the handler reference as the actor to receive all responses. But the code is much cleaner from having excised the anonymous actor implementation from the body of the `AccountBalanceRetriever`.

Despite the fact that we've created a new instance of the `AccountBalanceResponseHandler` for every request to get balances, I'm placing the `AccountBalanceRetriever`'s sender into a local variable in the receive block before passing it to the new instance of the `AccountBalanceResponseHandler`. Make certain you follow that pattern, since passing the sender `ActorRef` without first capturing it will expose your handler to the same problem (losing the sender of the message to whom we want to send our response) that we saw earlier where the sender `ActorRef` changed.

Also note that by using a "named" type, `AccountBalanceResponseHandler`, we'll have more useful information when debugging because anonymous types are assigned names in the JVM which aren't very easy to decipher. In my opinion, it is always preferrable to have named types over anonymous actors for this reason.

The Companion Object Factory Method

You may have noticed the comment in the `AccountBalanceResponseHandler` companion object that I now have defined a `props` method as a factory for my actor. See "The Companion Object Factory Method" on page 50 for more details about why I have done this.

How to Test This Logic

Testing this code is virtually identical to how we did it previously, and we can reuse the common stubs that we created as well. After we test the success case, we can inject a stub that will induce timeout to test the failure case:

```
import akka.testkit.{ TestKit, TestProbe, ImplicitSender }
import akka.actor.{ Actor, ActorLogging, ActorSystem, Props }
import org.scalatest.WordSpecLike
import org.scalatest.matchers.MustMatchers
import scala.concurrent.duration._
import org.jamieallen.effectiveakka.common._
import       org.jamieallen.effectiveakka.pattern.cameo.AccountBalanceResponseHandler._

class CameoSpec extends TestKit(ActorSystem("CameoTestAS"))
    with ImplicitSender with WordSpecLike with MustMatchers {

  val checkingAccountsProxy = system.actorOf(
    Props[CheckingAccountsProxyStub], "checkings")
  val moneyMarketAccountsProxy = system.actorOf(
    Props[MoneyMarketAccountsProxyStub], "money-markets")

  "An AccountBalanceRetriever" should {
    "return a list of account balances" in {
      val probe1 = TestProbe()
      val probe2 = TestProbe()
      val savingsAccountsProxy = system.actorOf(
        Props[SavingsAccountsProxyStub], "cameo-success-savings")
      val checkingAccountsProxy = system.actorOf(
        Props[CheckingAccountsProxyStub], "cameo-success-checkings")
      val moneyMarketAccountsProxy = system.actorOf(
        Props[MoneyMarketAccountsProxyStub], "cameo-success-money-markets")
      val accountBalanceRetriever = system.actorOf(
        Props(new AccountBalanceRetriever(savingsAccountsProxy,
                                          checkingAccountsProxy,
                                          moneyMarketAccountsProxy)),
                                          "cameo-retriever1")

      within(300 milliseconds) {
        probe1.send(accountBalanceRetriever, GetCustomerAccountBalances(1L))
        val result = probe1.expectMsgType[AccountBalances]
        result must equal(AccountBalances(
          Some(List((3, 15000))),
```

```
                Some(List((1, 150000), (2, 29000)))),
                Some(List())))
      }
      within(300 milliseconds) {
        probe2.send(accountBalanceRetriever, GetCustomerAccountBalances(2L))
        val result = probe2.expectMsgType[AccountBalances]
        result must equal(AccountBalances(
          Some(List((6, 640000), (7, 1125000), (8, 40000))),
          Some(List((5, 80000))),
          Some(List((9, 640000), (10, 1125000), (11, 40000)))))
      }
    }

    "return a TimeoutException when timeout is exceeded" in {
      val savingsAccountsProxy = system.actorOf(
        Props[TimingOutSavingsAccountProxyStub], "cameo-timing-out-savings")
      val checkingAccountsProxy = system.actorOf(
        Props[CheckingAccountsProxyStub], "cameo-timing-out-checkings")
      val moneyMarketAccountsProxy = system.actorOf(
        Props[MoneyMarketAccountsProxyStub], "cameo-timing-out-money-markets")
      val accountBalanceRetriever = system.actorOf(
        Props(new AccountBalanceRetriever(savingsAccountsProxy,
                                          checkingAccountsProxy,
                                          moneyMarketAccountsProxy)),
                                          "cameo-timing-out-retriever")
      val probe = TestProbe()

      within(250 milliseconds, 500 milliseconds) {
        probe.send(accountBalanceRetriever, GetCustomerAccountBalances(1L))
        probe.expectMsg(AccountRetrievalTimeout)
      }
    }
  }
}
```

When creating the stubs I use to inject mocks of services for the tests, I am *not* using the props() companion object for those actors. Can you see why? In this case, the instantiation of the Props instance for each stubbed actor is happening inside the context of a test, not another actor. So I don't have to worry about closing over "this" from the test context.

The cameo pattern allows you to be explicit about the type of the actor that will perform the work for each GetCustomerAccountBalances message sent to the AccountBalanceRetriever, which I generally prefer. I also think it separates concerns nicely, whereas the extra pattern can begin to make your code more difficult to read because of the amount of extra code it has inside of the body of the AccountBalanceRetriever.

CHAPTER 3

Best Practices

I have been fortunate enough to have been using Actors and Scala since 2009, but I have also experienced a great deal of pain from having made many mistakes in that time. Here are some important rules to follow for actor-based development, though many of the rules are applicable to asynchronous coding in general.

Actors Should Do Only One Thing

One of the hardest things to do in software development is to design a system based on primitives. By that, I mean the lowest level of functional decomposition we can achieve. With actors, we have the ability to define very elemental abstractions of functionality, and we want to take advantage of this. So how do we do it?

Single Responsibility Principle

Robert Martin, also known as "Uncle Bob," taught us in *Agile Software Development* (Prentice Hall) that we should try to isolate responsibilities into unique classes. In doing so, we avoid conflating what an object-oriented class should do and keep the implementation simple. Bob believes, and I agree with him, that each class should be concise and small, giving you more flexibility for its usage. The more you add to it that is outside of its base role, the more you have extra functionality and code for usages that may not require them.

With actors, I believe this to be particularly true. It is very easy to make an actor perform additional tasks—we simply add new messages to its receive block to allow it to perform more and different kinds of work. However, doing so limits your ability to compose systems of actors and define contextual groupings. Keep the actors focused on a single kind of work, and in doing so, allow yourself to use them flexibly.

Create Specific Supervisors

When we are building supervisor hierarchies, where we organize actors into trees of parents and children, it is easy to spawn children of multiple types (for example, under a `CustomerActor`, we could spawn `AccountActor` and `DeviceActor` instances) that share one `supervisorStrategy`. But this can be bad, because you only have one such strategy for each parent. There are some actor developers who feel this can largely be overcome by using very fine-grained exception types to communicate failure of children. However, because Akka only permits one strategy for each supervisor, there is no way to delineate between actors of one grouping for which `OneForOne` is the restart strategy you want, and another grouping for which `AllForOne` is the preferred restart strategy. Furthermore, because I believe in the Single Responsibility Principle, I want to separate logic unrelated from one another as much as possible. Let's look at an example.

`OneForOne` is a great strategy when the kind of failures that occur are specific to a single actor. This can be exceptions that occur when handling work passed in a message, or a runtime exception focused on a failure that would not affect other actors. `AllForOne` is a strategy you may want to employ when the kind of failure affects all of the actors under the supervisor, such as an exception connecting to a database in a child actor that will affect all—in this case, you can use `AllForOne` to stop all actors under the supervisor until the connection is known to have been reestablished.

In Figure 3-1, we have an error kernel that supervises two customers. The customer actors themselves supervise accounts and devices, and the accounts supervise the varying types of accounts we can have in our financial institution. Because I have accounts and devices under one supervisor, I have to define a single supervision strategy that is applicable to both. However, while I can design my `supervisorStrategy` failure handling to be common to both, I do not have the flexibility to introduce a different restart strategy for each of them. Now my system is more rigid and intractable.

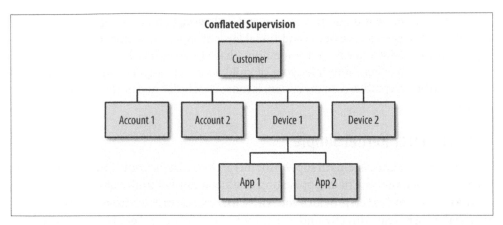

Figure 3-1. Conflated supervision

However, I can easily fix this problem by introducing a layer of supervision between the customer and accounts/devices children, as we see in Figure 3-2. In doing so, I can tailor supervision to be specific to failure that can occur with accounts and that which may occur with devices. Note that I don't have to do this for the varying kinds of accounts below the accounts actor: if I am comfortable that the varying types below a supervisor are sufficiently similar, there is likely no need to add the extra overhead of more supervision layers.

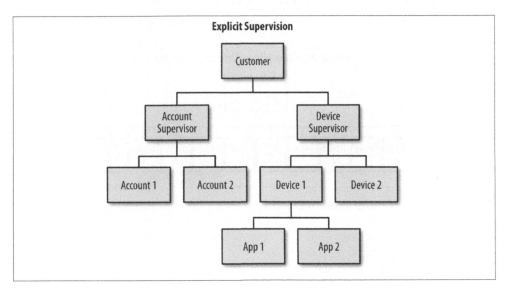

Figure 3-2. Explicit supervision

The counter argument might be that you end up having to do more upward escalation of failure messages because of the additional layer of supervision introduced by following this pattern. But since it's not something I have to do everywhere in my supervisor hierarchies (only where multiple types of child actors are supervised by one actor), I find that to be acceptable. And my system is more clearly defined in elemental, primitive terms.

Keep the Error Kernel Simple

It is a pattern of actor systems in supervisor hierarchies that the root of the trees compose an error kernel, the part of an application that must not fail under any circumstances. And Akka's ActorSystem provides you with a *user guardian* actor to supervise all actors you as the user create directly under that root of the ActorSystem. However, you have no programmatic control over the user guardian. It merely specifies that for any java.lang.Exception that percolates up to it, all actors under it are restarted.

Look at the way our actors are organized in Figure 3-3. The problem with flat hierarchies is that any kind of AllForOne restarting supervision would result in a lot of actors being restarted, potentially when they were completely unaffected by the error that occurred. It can be tempting to put many different kinds of actors directly under the guardian. Don't. Instead, build layers of failure handling that isolate failure deep in the tree so that as few actors as possible are affected by something going wrong. Never be afraid to introduce layers of actors if it makes your supervisor hierarchy more clear and explicit, as we see in Figure 3-4.

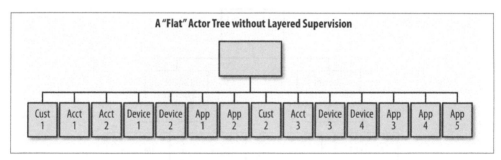

Figure 3-3. Flat actor supervisor hierarchy

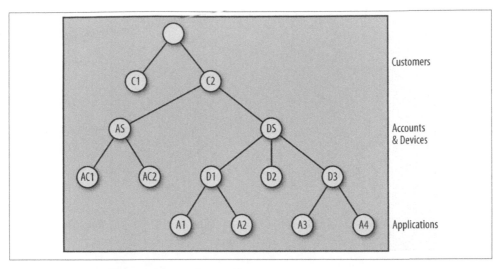

Customers

Accounts
& Devices

Applications

Figure 3-4. Deep actor supervisor hierarchy

Creating shallow actor hierarchies with a substantial number of actors should be a "smell test" to you. The deeper your hierarchies, the more you can compose layers to handle failures that can occur. If you have a shallow hierarchy, you are likely not defining the problems that can occur in your problem domain well enough. Think about whether or not failures can be made more granular and how you can layer failure into specific, well-isolated branches within the tree.

Failure Zones

When we build trees of actors, it is a common mistake to continually use the default dispatcher provided to you as part of an ActorSystem. And when you're just getting started or trying to prototype something, that can be fine. However, when you're creating a supervisor hierarchy for a production actor-based application, you want to limit the impact of what happens in one grouping of actors with any others. How do we do this? Let's look at a supervision tree using only the default dispatcher of the ActorSystem, as shown in Figure 3-5.

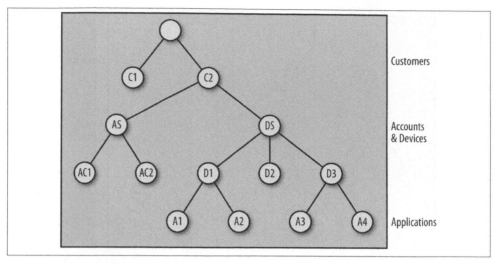

Customers

Accounts
& Devices

Applications

Figure 3-5. No failure zones

In this case, we have our banking customer supervision hierarchy. We have an error kernel managing customers, who in turn are supervising accounts and devices. However, because we haven't explicitly created any of the actors with any other dispatchers, any kind of expensive computation or blocking that takes place in one part of the hierarchy can lead to actor starvation in another actor that is completely unrelated. That, of course, would be bad.

Instead, we want to build groupings of actors in our supervisor hierarchy that should share resources such as thread pools, as we see in Figure 3-6. In doing so, we allow the failure that can take place in one part of the system to have no bearing on any other unrelated component.

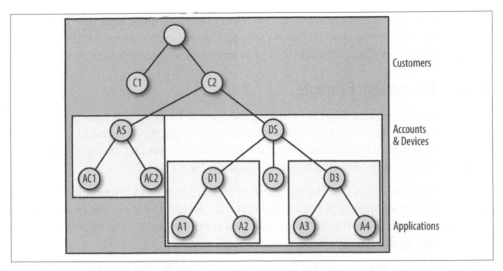

Figure 3-6. With failure zones

That said, Martin Thompson, and, by extension, Gary Player, developed a measure called *Mechanical Sympathy*, where you as the developer must understand how hardware works to get the most out of it. The measure must be applied when defining dispatchers. Make sure you think about the following items:

1. What kinds of machines, with how many cores, will run this application?

2. How CPU-bound are the tasks being performed by my actors?

3. How many threads can I realistically expect to run concurrently for this application on those machines?

The answers to those questions are highly specific to your application and how it runs. Just keep in mind that it makes no sense to define hundreds of dispatchers with thousands of threads if the tasks are CPU-bound. Try it out on your work machine, and you'll find that actors are starving for resources not because you didn't define enough threads for them to use, but because they couldn't get enough CPU time to take advantage of those resources.

Avoid Blocking

One of the worst offenders when creating high-throughput applications on the JVM is blocking threads. By blocking the thread, you allow the kernel executing the thread to release it from its core, which introduces context switching and the resultant loss of "warmed" caches local to that core. Even if the thread is rescheduled quickly, it is plausible that it will be on another core and data for the thread will have to be reloaded from main memory. This introduces additional latency, as the instructions to be executed have to wait for the data required to be processed. It is difficult to quantify the cost of a context switch, as it varies across hardware and kernel combinations, but it is not unreasonable to assert that a context switch has an overhead of several microseconds.

Futures Delegation Example

So how do we avoid blocking? By allowing the logic to be delegated to a future, which can execute in another context—a new thread, returning a new value and allowing us to define behavior that can be executed *at that time*. Is this as fast as sequential operations? Absolutely not. However it is more scalable. Here's how.

Actors receive messages into their mailboxes and process them sequentially. There is no question of concurrency in actors, and that is by design. We are using an abstraction to provide us with the ability to write code that is purely declarative. It only describes what we want to do.

But, by definition, that means that the actor can only handle one message at a time and therefore is limited by the amount of work that must be accomplished in handling that message. If we do nothing to change that execution model, the actor could conceivably be overwhelmed by the time it takes to handle messages relative to the number of messages being enqueued.

The answer is to perform the behavior dictated by the received message in futures. In doing so, the actor is able to receive a message, define the work that must be accomplished to successfully handle the request, and then immediately handle the next message in its mailbox and do the same thing. We *delegate* the work to be performed at some time in the future and define how to handle the success or failure of that task. And this works because the actor is stateless, aside from the `DatabaseDriver` in use:

```
case object TransactionSuccess

class CustomerUpdater(dbDriver: DatabaseDriver) extends Actor {
  def receive = {
    case UpdateCustomer(customer) =>
      val originalSender = sender
      implicit val ec: ExecutionContext =
        ExecutionContext.fromExecutor(new ForkJoinPool())
      val future = Future {
        // define some JDBC action
      }

      future.onCompletion(
        case Failure(x) => throw new CustomerUpdateException(x)
        case Success => originalSender ! TransactionSuccess()
      )
  }
}
```

In this case, the actor is responsible for performing updates to customer records in a database. It receives messages to update a customer record, passing the new customer information. It then performs the database transaction via the database driver passed to it. In most cases, you would use a pool of such actors, much like a connection pool, so that you don't have to spin up new instances of database transaction actors every time you want to do work, and no one is overloaded.

The key here is that the actor receives the update request. It uses a future to delegate the work to the `transactionActor`, and defines what to do if a failure occurs, such as a `SQLException`, by throwing a new, more specific exception back to its supervisor. It wraps the information about the failure and allows the supervisor to determine what happened and what should be done as a result.

But that's not the important thing to take away from this. What's important is that we've defined all of this work to take place asynchronously, without blocking any threads. The actor defines this behavior and then is free to handle the next message in its mailbox. The latency associated with the database interaction is no longer a factor in the actor's ability to handle messages.

Think about defining a separate dispatcher for your futures so that you do not impact the message handling by actors. If you use the same dispatcher as the actors, you can have the same starvation issues you were trying to avoid by off-loading the work to another thread to begin with. Give thought to the execution context that should be used by each component in your asynchronous system.

Java futures are blocking!

A quick digression before we continue. One thing I am continually amazed about is how few people know or understand the Java Future API. There are only five methods you can call an instance of a `java.util.concurrent.Future` class, and only two of those are relevant to getting the expected data out of it.

First, you have `get()`. This method blocks the current thread until a future instance completes its work, thus requiring the use of one thread more than the work that must be performed just to manage what happens when it is done. Second, you have `is Done()`, which merely allows you to define other work and check to see if the Future is completed. Either way, the calling thread must continue to do work or make itself do a busy spin until *both* futures complete. This is a horrible waste of resources!

Think about it. If you have two tasks you want to be performed asynchronously, you have to define that work from a calling thread in two separate futures. You then have to make the calling thread block on `get()` or perform busy spin in a while loop until `isDone()` returns true. It is taking three threads to do the work of two.

However, if you use `scala.concurrent.Future` (or the `akka.util.Futures` API for Java), you can define work to be performed asynchronously, as well as the behavior to manage what happens when it is done or fails, and then release the calling thread. Threads are valuable resources, as are cores. We should not be wasting them on house-keeping, but the current Java Future API does just that.

It is possible that Doug Lea will work his magic and have a Java implementation of CompletableFuture ready for Java 8, but it's impossible to say, at the time I write this, whether that will be ready in time for the code freeze.

Pre-defining Parallel Futures

The Scala Future API allows us to pre-define work and then stage the way that work is handled via nested Future instances. If you want to create a pair of futures to run in parallel, you do so independently and then use a for comprehension to handle the results. However, this only works when the results are unrelated and not dependent on one to complete before the next can be handled.

For example, imagine we wanted to display information on a stock trading web page. The customer has selected the security she wishes to purchase. We need to find out the current bid, ask prices, find out the price the security trade for last, and then return that to the view layer to be composed into a response and returned to the customer. We first define the Future instances to get both pieces of information, and then we define the behavior for handling the results:

```scala
class SecurityPricingActor(exchange: Exchange,
                           backOffice: BackOffice) extends Actor {
  def receive = {
    case GetPricingInfo(security: Security) =>
      val originalSender = sender
      val bidAndAskFuture = Future { exchange.getBidAndAsk(security.id) }
      val lastPriceFuture = Future { backOffice.getLastPrice(security.id) }

      val response = for {
        (bid, ask) = bidAndAskFuture
        lastPrice = lastPriceFuture
      } yield SecurityPricing(bid, ask, lastPrice)
      response map (originalSender ! _)
  }
}
```

It is important to understand the dynamics at play here. We define two futures to get information from two external services. We then define a for comprehension that will monadically bind the behavior of what to do when both values are returned. However, the for comprehension is syntactic sugar for the flatMap and map methods on the future instance, and just like those methods, intermediate future instances are returned.

So consider the implications of that. The type of response is a Future[SecurityPricing]. However, the result of the bidAndAskFuture is a Future[BigDecimal, BigDecimal]. If and only if that returns successfully do we get a new Future[BigDecimal] for the `lastPrice`. And if and only if that succeeds is the `Future[SecurityPricing]` going to be evaluated. But the expensive tasks, which may involve going over some wire to get the information from the exchange or another external service, is not blocking the calling thread, nor is the behavior defined about what to do when they complete.

Parallel Futures with the zip() Method

There is another syntax for performing `Future` execution in parallel, and that is the use of the `zip()` method in the Future API. This allows you to get around defining the futures outside of the `for` comprehension, and some people perfer the syntax. For conciseness, I agree that this is cleaner. However, I find that predefining my futures is more expressive and allows my `for` comprehension to be more readable, so I usually eschew this style:

```
class SecurityPricingActor(exchange: Exchange,
                           backOffice: BackOffice) extends Actor {
  def receive = {
    case GetPricingInfo(security: Security) =>
      val originalSender = sender

      val response = for {
        ((bid, ask), lastPrice) = Future {
            exchange.getBidAndAsk(security.id)
          } zip Future {
            backOffice.getLastPrice(security.id)
          }
      } yield SecurityPricing(bid, ask, lastPrice)
      response map (originalSender ! _)
  }
}
```

Sequential Futures

What can be particularly tricky is understanding how to compose the use of futures. Sometimes, work cannot be performed entirely in parallel and must be executed in a particular order, due to a dependency between the values returned from multiple calls.

For example, imagine you used a future to get a set of customers from a database, and then wanted to call another external service to get account information for each customer. How would you predefine that behavior so that you didn't have to block the calling thread? The answer is to use `for` comprehensions and embed the work to be performed in the futures inside of the structure of the `for` comprehension so that the second future was only executed if the first one successfully returned the value upon which it depended:

```
val accountsForCustomers = for {
  customer <- Future { databaseService.getCustomers }
```

```
        account <- Future { accountService.getAccounts(customer.id) }
    } yield (customer, account)
```

Callbacks versus Monadic Handling

So far, we have used the callback style (onSuccess, onFailure, onComplete) as well as the monadic style (for comprehensions) for handling the result of future instances. You may wonder why there are two different syntaxes and when to use each. By convention, the callback style is to be used for side-effecting responses, such as the database access call in the CustomerUpdater example. The monadic style is for "pure" functional representations, free of side-effecting code. Anyone familiar with functional programming and the desire for purity will likely recognize the pattern.

However, note that the callback style can be unwieldy if we need to nest futures and their result-handling callbacks. We want to be able to compose our logic in a meaningful way, and using for comprehensions allow us to compose how we handle the results of multiple futures in a clear, succinct way.

Futures and ExecutionContext

While the Future API is very handy for defining work to take place asynchronously, they require an ExecutionContext in order to perform their tasks. This ExecutionContext provides a thread pool from which they draw their required resources. Many people start off by using the ActorSystem default dispatcher like so:

```
val system = ActorSystem()
implicit val ec: ExecutionContext = system.dispatcher
Future { /* work to be performed */ }
```

However, using the ActorSystem's default dispatcher can lead to thread starvation very quickly if it becomes overloaded with potential work. The default configuration of this dispatcher is to be elastically sized from 8 to 64 threads. So just as we saw when discussing failure zones, we should consider it important to isolate execution by context.

You can similarly use an actor's dispatcher. This gives you more resource granularity but still requires your actor to dedicate a thread to the future every time one is instantiated. This also might not be ideal:

```
implicit val ec: ExecutionContext = context.dispatcher
Future { /* work to be performed */ }
```

You always have the option of creating a new ExecutionContext from a new thread pool on the fly, which can be done like so:

```
implicit val ec: ExecutionContext =
    ExecutionContext.fromExecutor(new ForkJoinPool())
Future { /* work to be performed */ }
```

However, a best practice I recommend is that you consider when you may want to define specific dispatchers inside the configuration of each ActorSystem in which futures will be used. Then you can dynamically apply the dispatcher for use in your code, like this:

```
implicit val ec: ExecutionContext = context.system.dispatchers.lookup("foo")
Future { /* work to be performed */ }
```

Push, Don't Pull

It is common for developers new to Akka, and actors in general, to want to control the flow of actor interactions by "asking" another actor for a response. This may seem fine from the outset, but as you mature as an actor developer, you have to take into consideration the cost of doing such a thing. First of all, the ask pattern in Akka requires a future to send the message in the first place, and queues a callback or monadic handler for the response with the ExecutionContext. It also has a timeout associated with it.

All of these combine to be quite heavy for a simple actor interaction that could be as simple as sending a message and being prepared to handle the response. Furthermore, you are making assumptions about time in your system, saying that you expect a response within a certain timeframe, and you have to design what to do when that interaction does not take place.

It is better to instead use *fire and forget* semantics for such interactions. It is lighter weight and makes no assumptions about what must happen at what time. For resilience, your best bet is to actually become a handler for a specific response and then schedule a send starting right at that moment to repeat every so many seconds until a response is received, at which point the send is cancelled:

```
object MyActor {
  case class DataToHandle(bytes: Array[Byte])
  case object GetData
}
class MyActor(otherActor: ActorRef) extends Actor {
  import MyActor._
  import context.dispatcher

  var cancellable: Option[Cancellable] = None
  def receive = {
    case Start =>
      context.become(dataHandler)
      cancellable = Some(context.system.scheduler.
        schedule(0 milliseconds, 500 milliseconds, otherActor, GetData))
  }

  def dataHandler: Receive = {
    case DataToHandle(data) =>
      // Do something
      cancellable map (_.cancel)
      context.unbecome
```

```
      }
   }
```

You might question whether this is a good idea, as the MyActor instance will now not handle any Start messages received until a DataToHandle message is received. In some cases, this may be what you want. However, if you need to handle more Start messages, you should use the extra or cameo patterns to define a new actor instance to handle what to do when the response is finally received.

Another option is to *chain* your receive messages, where you allow an actor to register receive blocks and handle the messages received in an ordered fashion because the traits used are linearized (as traits are wont to be). This is accomplished by pre-pending them to the list of receives you manage, like so:[1]

```
trait ChainingActor extends Actor {
  private var chainedReceives: List[Receive] = List()

  def registerReceive(newReceive: Receive) {
    chainedReceives = newReceive :: chainedReceives
  }

  def receive = chainedReceives.reduce(_ orElse _)
}

trait IntActor extends ChainingActor {
  registerReceive {
    case i: Int => println("Int!")
  }
}

trait StringActor extends ChainingActor {
  registerReceive {
    case s: String => println("String!")
  }
}
```

Another aspect to consider is that if all of your interactions stem from making calls until an appropriate response is received, it won't matter that each actor is ignoring the other messages because it will receive each message multiple times. This is critical for building resilient systems! Never expect guarantees of delivery for any message over any medium, regardless of whether or not you know you're sending messages within a JVM or using Durable Mailboxes or a middleware message broker that supposedly will persist messages. Failures can happen anywhere: in your application, in the hardware, or over the network.

---

1. This idea was gleaned from Dan Simon, as explained in the post on StackOverflow (*http://bit.ly/1exCzCF*).

Resilient systems make no expectations about "guarantees" and always keep trying to do what they need to do until it gets done and they're sure of it.

When You Must Block

While it would be ideal to not block threads, the reality is that there will be times when you must perform a blocking operation. A great example is any time an actor is going to perform database work via a legacy database driver. And that's fine—there is no way for you to communicate with such an external resource and receive a reply without blocking.

The key is to make sure that you limit the effect of the blocking call. To do that, you should put any such actor (or multiple actors in a router) with blocking calls inside of its own dispatcher with resources that aren't shared by any other actors that perform nonblocking work. By isolating the blocking calls to actors that don't share resources with others, we can be sure that other actors won't be starved for a thread within the JVM while the blocking actor does its work:

```
// Code from an actor that will create the blocking actor
val customerRetriever = context.actorOf(Props[CustomerRetrievalActor].
                        withDispatcher("customer-retrieval-dispatcher"),
                        "customer-retriever")

// Blocking actor pseudocode
class CustomerRetrievalActor extends Actor {
  def receive = {
    case GetCustomer(id) =>
      // Make a database call to look up a customer by the ID sent
  }
}
```

Managed Blocking in Scala

Scala has a very handy feature called *Managed Blocking* for controlling the amount of blocking code that can exist within an application. When you wrap a block of code with blocking, the thread pool upon which the code will run is notified that the task is blocking or long-running. That thread pool can then elastically spawn and remove additional threads to ensure that no actor or future sharing it is starved for a thread. See Managed Blocking in the Scala documentation for more information:

```
import scala.concurrent.blocking
blocking {
  // Do some blocking behavior
}
```

There is a caveat here, of course. Yes, it is great that you can get more threads if blocked threads are consuming your thread pool. However, they are not capped at a specific limit. It is theoretically possible that you can expand the size of your thread pool limitlessly, and that could quickly use up a lot of resources. Keep this in mind when you use managed blocking, and think about how you can use circuit breakers or some other mechanism to provide backpressure when the system is being overwhelmed.

Avoid Premature Optimization

As a side note, I tell people in my "Effective Actors" presentation never to parallelize with routers before you have measured the hot spots in your application. Too often, developers (including myself) make assumptions about where we expect performance to be slow and try to mitigate those problems up front.

Be careful not to create routers before you have proven at runtime under load that you absolutely need to. If you suspect you will need to use a router somewhere, Akka team leader Roland Kuhn recommends that you pass around actor references from supervisors to compute-intensive children so that the context.parent of their children are free to become a router later on merely by changing the external configuration of the actor.

Start Simple

When designing your Akka application, try to model the interactions in as simple a way as possible. By that, I mean try not to think in terms of asynchronous interactions or how specific algorithms will be designed. Instead, think in terms of the flow of the application, and where possible, try to direct it toward a result.

When I started building actor-based applications, we had teams responsible for building individual subsystems that flowed from one to another. Each subsystem consisted of a RESTful API, a domain, and a real-time component where side effects resulting from the commit of data to the database would be realized. Inside of that real-time realm, we had to model what to do as a result of a new domain object being added, removed, or changed. We did not focus on the details, just what had to be accomplished for each event.

To build an actor-based system from scratch, try to follow this roadmap, as defined by Jonas Bonér.

Deterministic

Try to think in terms of your application being entirely synchronous in nature. This can be tricky, since designing an application to be asynchronous does require that you think about the problem differently than a synchronous application, where you expect a definitive order of execution. But if you can think about your problem as if you have those guarantees, start there. Worry about nondeterministic behavior once you have defined your problem and how the logic would flow if it were synchronous.

When I wrote my first actor-based system, we were attempting to manage the realization of domain types to multiple servers in a cluster: if someone created a customer, we wanted to create a `Customer` actor whose sole responsibility was to make sure all servers for whom that customer should exist were able to update themselves with the customer's information. In this case, we could reason about what would happen in the asynchronous part of our application pretty easily: if you added a domain object, it would result in that domain object being "realized" to a server in our cluster. Assuming no failure and not taking into account timing issues, the add succeeded, and our system was in a nominal state. If failure or timing issues (such as the customer being added before type on which it depended) occurred, the actor continued attempting to realize that domain object until it succeeded.

Declarative

This applies to nonactor applications as well. When writing Scala, we want to focus on being as declarative as possible—focus on *what* you want to do, not *how* it will be done. Imperative programming in Java is nondeclarative. When we want to iterate over a collection and get out only those values that meet some criteria and put the values into a new collection, we have to write the code like this (assuming we're not using a nonstandard language library):

```
List shortWords = new ArrayList();
for (String word : wordList)
{
    if (word.length < 5)
    {
        shortWords.add(word);
    }
}
```

In Scala, we instead focus on what we want to do so that the details of how that work is done don't clutter the logic of our application:

```
val shortWords = wordList.filter(_.length < 5)
```

This makes our code considerably more concise, which means that it is cognitively easier for someone else maintaining our code to understand what is going on and make changes to it with confidence. We want developers to be able to understand semantically what is happening in our application as quickly as possible and not be bogged down in details of how things are being accomplished.

Immutable

Like declarative programming, we want to focus on immutability regardless of whether or not we're writing Akka applications. But the reason it is so important with actors and futures is that your application will be multithreaded by nature. By focusing on immutability, you are ensuring correctness of data shared across threads and reducing the possibility of dead locks or live locks that can occur when using locks to manage shared, mutable state.

Functional

Again, this is a rule for non-Akka application development as well, and it's somewhat redundant to the immutability just mentioned. By functional, I mean your code should be immutable, referentially transparent, and have first-class functions. Actors themselves are not functional programming constructs, but we do want to adhere to these principles within the actors as much as possible. Referential transparency is when you can substitute a value for a block of code and still have the exact same result: no side effects have taken place, and no unintended consequences of the evaluation of those expressions exist. First-class functions mean they can be passed as arguments to methods, just like a string or a domain object, or they could be composed functionally (such as through for comprehensions).

Keep mutability and side effects *within* the actor, and favor vars of immutable data. For example, because actors prevent concurrent access to internal mutable state, it is easy to use mutable data structures. However, if you decide to pass that data elsewhere, you've created a concurrency issue. It is better to use vars of *immutable* data structures inside of actors so you do not have to worry about that.

Layer in Complexity via Indeterminism

Once you have built your application following the the functional paradigm, you want to begin to attack the problem in targeted locations where you've measured that you need to increase performance. How do we do that? Identify the parts of your system where additional asynchrony will have the most benefit: for example, blocking I/O or anywhere you've actually measured a critical section that can't handle the load. From there, layer in additional asynchrony via anonymous actors and futures only in those targeted spots.

Optimize with Mutability

Now you have an application that is functional and asynchronous. This is very desirable, but the nature of functional programming is that it results in the creation of lots of (hopefully) short-lived objects on the JVM. That is okay: if the lifespan of such objects is limited to Eden in the JVM's garbage collection regions. However, if they begin to leak into OldGen, they will be costly to clean up and could result in lots of compaction latency. So, in order to optimize our application, we may begin to look at mutable state *in very targeted locations, where we have proven with measurements obtained from profiling our application at runtime,* to make our code run more efficiently. How can we do that?

Add mutability with compare and swap (CAS)

This is where things start to get tricky. You've built your asynchronous system, and it meets your requirements for what it is supposed to do. However, you're finding that it isn't able to perform the work as quickly as your nonfunctional requirements dictate, and parallelism isn't an option because you don't have a task that can be performed independently and concurrently on different JVMs. You need to optimize your code. One way to do so is to use mutable state.

However, using mutable state can be very tricky. You want to avoid locking as much as you possibly can, and not just because of the difficulty of managing locks programmatically. Locks, even on an abstracted platform such as the JVM, are arbitrated by the kernel of the OS on which the JVM is running. This means that lock access happens on a core executing the kernel, and your thread is paused to arbitrate lock access. When this happens, the core can be assigned a new thread, and the data specific to your thread in the warmed caches local to that core is now evicted for the data required by the new thread. This can have a measurable affect on performance, because even if your thread was scheduled back to that same core, it is extremely likely that you will encounter cache misses, and the data your thread needs will have to be reloaded from main memory.

In order to avoid this, we can use Java's excellent Atomic References. These use compare and swap (CAS) semantics to discern if a change can be made to the data it protects by comparing the data to be changed with what it expects the data should still be, assuming no other changes have taken place, at the time the change will occur. If I use an `Atomi cInteger` to wrap a counter, and I want to increment the value from 5 to 6, the change will fail if the counter is not a value of 5 at the time I'm effecting the change. Java 8 is adding new `Adder` and `Accumulator` types that will greatly facilitate this, if you have the ability to run with that platform.

Compose CAS with Software Transactional Memory

This will only get you so far, however, as Java's Atomic References do not compose. By that, I mean you cannot combine two `AtomicInteger` instances to have one atomic operation. To do this, you can use *Software Transactional Memory* (STM), where you make changes to the two values within the context of a single transaction, and the commit only occurs if both values are what was expected at the time the commit takes place.

However, STM is not some magical awesome-sauce that you spread around your application that makes things just magically start working. If the data upon which you apply STM is changing rapidly via other threads, it is entirely possible that the memory cannot be committed as collisions in the multifield CAS operations aren't occurring fast enough to compensate for the changes occurring. It is a tool that is available to you but has its limitations.

As a side note, one very nice feature of Scala-STM is the TMap collection, which can provide you snapshots of the collection's data in constant time. That can be a handy feature on some situations. For more information, see the documentation (*http://nbron son.github.io/scala-stm/*).

Add locks as a last resort

As an absolute last resort, such as when CAS-semantics do not work for your application because updates to the data are happening too quickly, resulting in too many failures to effect changes, you have to use locks. But only do so as an absolute last resort. This is why you were most likely looking at building an actor-based system to begin with.

Locks do not compose, so trying to interleave them can easily lead to deadlock and live lock situations. Deadlocks are at least relatively easy to find, identified via jstack's listing of threads in the JVM or JConsole/VisualVM. Live locks are much trickier because both threads involved are actively doing work but unable to get out of each others' way. Think of it as being analogous to walking down a street where someone is coming in the opposite direction, and both of you keep stepping in the same direction and can't get out of the way of one another.

Furthermore, *mutually exclusive locks* (MUTEXs) are very expensive when they are contended. Blocked threads are removed from the core one which they are executing by the operating system kernel so that other threads have a chance to run. Even if the contended lock gets access quickly, it has to be rescheduled by the kernel and may not be placed back on the same core. All of the warmed hardware caches local to that core are now lost and must be rebuilt where the thread continues its execution.

Prepare for Race Conditions

With asynchronous code (such as Akka actors), we gain tremendous benefits from being able to leverage threads and maximize the usage of physical hardware resources such as cores and sockets. However, this comes at the expense of determinism, the guarantee that providing the same inputs will always result in the same logic path being executed and the same result. This means that it is entirely plausible, or even likely, that we will experience race conditions, where we expect something to have a specific value at a particular time, but it does not.

Avoid coding in a way where timing matters

So how do we avoid writing code that is dependent on time? This goes back to my core belief that resilient systems never try to do things only once: they continue to do things until the world around them changes to the way they expect it to be, or they escalate failure so that higher-level supervisors can recognize that the world needs to be pushed in a particular direction. If you write asynchronous code, such as Akka actors, with the expectation that everything will always happen at just the right time, you are going to fail pretty quickly.

Here is an example. While working at a large cable company, we were building a repository of what channels every customer was allowed to watch, based on what they were paying for. A customer could call in at any time and change those permissions, and those changes had to be reflected in the data set within 10 minutes. The "source of truth" database could provide the information, but the relational queries involved too many joins to be performant enough to meet our nonfunctional requirements for servicing requests. We came up with two possible solutions:

1. Every day, a master file of all reference data was reloaded from external sources. We would create a system to poll the "source of truth" database providing all customer information and then resolve who could watch what channels and load them into a live cache. That cache would be updated all day long with new information if a customer's account changed. However, this is a time-based system: if we missed an event or if an exception occurred trying to handle a single record, it was possible that the entire live cache of data would no longer be in synch with the database, requiring a complete reload, which could take over two hours, during which time viewing rights could not easily be enforced.

2. Alternatively, we could create a grouping of Akka actors that were each responsible for a hashed set of customer accounts. At the beginning of their iteration through a set of customers, they would retrieve all reference data from the database and all updates to customer accounts. They would then cycle through all customer accounts relevant to their hash, recalculate the viewing permissions for each, and place the data into the live cache. When they reached the end of their set, they restarted their cycle. If failure occurred mid-cycle, the supervisor could ask for all reference data and customer updates and restart the actor. This is a solution that is completely independent of time, where the data is self-healing with a worst-case scenario of being out of synch with the "source of truth" for whatever the amount of time it took to completely recycle through the set of accounts. This is a resilient solution providing eventual consistency that is agnostic to time. I call these kinds of actors "sentinels," as they guard the system from falling out of synchrony with a known expectation of what state should exist in the system.

Try to think of how you can approach your problem similarly. It may be easier to first think about the problem in terms of your blocking, time-based approach. But once you've properly identified what you have to do, you can think about the same problem in terms of how to implement it such that time doesn't matter and the system can heal itself.

Tell, don't ask

A best practice for actor development is to avoid ask: use fire and forget messages, and be prepared to handle responses. This is simpler and more expressive than using futures and having to map over composed responses, but I'm also only using one asynchronous threaded resource (the anonymous actor I created) as opposed to multiple futures for the sends and the myriad futures returned within a composed for comprehension to handle the results. Always try to focus on tell over ask.

Truly fault-resilient systems send messages in fire and forget fashion and prepare to receive the expected response. They do not make assumptions that sending once means that the message was definitely received and is being handled, since anything can happen in between. As such, we should schedule a task to continually resend that message a pre-defined number of times in some acceptable duration. If no expected response is received within that timeframe, we should be able to handle or escalate the failure.

Be Explicit

One of the surest ways to get yourself into trouble when using actors is by being vague or general in your interactions. Instead, you want to make sure that you have well-defined interactions and know exactly what failures can occur. This way, you can minimize the impact on other actors at runtime and keep "event storms" from happening, which can be very difficult to reason about.

Name Actors and ActorSystem Instances

First of all, give unique names to all of your actors and ActorSystem instances. Not only will this allow you to create and update external configuration for those objects on the fly after the fact, but you will be able to write code that references them by name via actor lookup. If you don't name them, you will have to add names later on when you decide you do want to do these things. Furthermore, you'll find more information in the Akka trace logs and logging when you name them:

```
// Create with name
val myActor = context.actorOf(Props[MyActor], "my-actor")

// Lookup
val myActor = context.system.actorFor("my-actor")
```

Note that, as of Akka 2.2, the old actorFor method has been deprecated due to differences in behavior between actors found locally versus those that are remote. Instead, use actorSelection, which looks up actors via absolute or relative paths. See the Akka documentation (*http://bit.ly/17cudgQ*) for more details.

Create Specialized Messages

Make a point to avoid passing messages that are general and do not get targeted toward a specific actor instance. You want your messages to flow through your supervisor hierarchy in a direct fashion, routing to the actor instance that is best equipped to handle the message without being sent down to others outside of its path. Here is an example of a generic message that you do not want to send through your supervisor hierarchy:

```
case object AccountsUpdated
```

This is a general message that will have to go to every `CustomerActor` in your system, and all of them will have to determine if that message is relevant to them. This is how event storms can occur, as all of your customers need to figure out from some service whether or not they care about this event.

Instead, we want to send messages that are very explicit so that only the `CustomerActor` for which the account changed is notified and performs work based upon the message. Here is an example of an explicit message:

```
case class AccountRemoved(customerId: Long, accountId: Long)
```

Create Specialized Exceptions

When creating supervisor hierarchies, it is tempting to try to generalize exception handling so that you can catch virtually every possible failure at the lowest possible level. However, this defeats the purpose of escalating failure to the appropriate level. What do I mean be generalizing exceptions?

```
class MySupervisor extends Actor {
  override val supervisorStrategy =
    OneForOneStrategy() {
      case _: Exception => Restart
    }
    ...
}
```

In this case, our supervisor is going to restart every individual actor it is supervising when any exception is thrown from them. But this is the default supervision behavior provided by Akka if you do not override it, so it's actually redundant! But that does not mean we should ever omit it.

If you do not override the default `supervisorStrategy` in your supervisor actor, the default behavior will be to escalate the failure upwards. If there is no handler all the way to the root of your supervision hierarchy, the "root guardian" actor in Akka, which is supervising your hierarchy within its `ActorSystem` context, will catch it and automatically restart everything below! While this can be useful for restarting a system that has suffered a catastrophic failure, it is hardly the default behavior you likely want for your application. Akka will handle a few exceptions it knows about explicitly, but everything else will just be result in the restarting of all of your actors.

 By default, Akka will stop a child actor on `ActorInitializationEx` `ception` and `ActorKilledException`. Akka will restart a child actor on `Exception`, and all other types will be escalated to the parent actor.

Think about what that would mean. You have a reasonably benign failure somewhere deep in your supervision hierarchy. That failure bubbles up to the `ActorSystem`, resulting in all of the actors you created in that `ActorSystem` being restarted when they finish handling their current messages. Whatever transient state they may have had would be lost, and all because of something that could have been handled more locally.

The better route is to create very specific exception types at the leaves of your supervision tree. As you flow upward, the exception types defined can be more general, and escalation can be used to make sure the appropriate supervisor ends up handling the message:

```
class MySupervisor extends Actor {
  override val supervisorStrategy =
    OneForOneStrategy() {
      case _: SQLException => Resume
      case _: MyDbConnectionException => Escalate
    }
    ...
}
```

In this case, the `SQLException` was probably related to bad data in the message being processed to update the database. How you handle such problems is domain-specific to your application: maybe you need to tell the user, maybe retry the message that was handled, etc. But a connection problem may be indicative of something that may be an issue for all actors trying to access that data store, such as a network partition. Then again, it might not be, if it is related to an authentication issue. In this case, you want to escalate the failure to the parent actor responsible for managing all actors with such database connections, which can decide whether this was an isolated failure or one of many occurring simultaneously. If the latter, it may decide to stop all actors relying on those connections until a new connection can be established.

Beware the "Thundering Herd"

One of the drawbacks of using general messages and exceptions is that they can lead to the unintended consequence of too much activity taking place in your actor application, too many messages being sent around as a result, or too many actors being affected by something that could have been handled locally. When this happens, you see "event storms" that can be difficult to diagnose. Tons of log output to pore over, lots of messages in the event trace logs of Akka, etc. It is entirely plausible that, despite your best intentions, such storms could happen anyway, as it is highly unlikely you'll think of every possible event that could lead to such a happening from the outset. But there are a couple of ways to handle them.

Dampen message overload

If you know that your system is capable of sending messages in a repeated fashion over and over again in an effort to provide resiliency, you have to be able to ignore the same message that may arrive again after you've already handled it. One such pattern I've seen, based on basic control theory, is to dampen your messages by a unique identifier. If you have received a message with the same such ID within the past x number of milliseconds, simply ignore it.

Use circuit breakers for failure overload

This is a feature for handling cascading failures in remote endpoints of your distributed application. You merely define that you want to implement this behavior, and provide inputs for how many failures can occur in how much time and how long to wait before reopening the circuit breaker:

```
class CircuitBreakingActor extends Actor {
  import context.dispatcher

  val circuitBreaker = new CircuitBreaker(context.system.scheduler,
                       maxFailures = 10,
                       callTimeout = 100.milliseconds,
                       resetTimeout = 1.seconds).
                         onOpen(logCircuitBreakerOpen())

  def logCircuitBreakerOpen() = log.info("CircuitBreaker is open")
```

Using circuit breakers allows you to provide fast failure semantics to services and clients. For example, if they were sending a RESTful request to your system, they wouldn't have to wait for their request to time out to know that they've failed, since the circuit breaker will report failure immediately.

Don't Expose Actors

Actors are intended to be self-contained components that do not have any interactions with the outside world except via their mailboxes. As such, they should never, ever be treated in the same fashion that you would an ordinary class.

Prior to the creation of the `ActorRef` proxy for Akka actors, it was entirely plausible to be able to create an actor and send it a message but also directly call a method on it as well. This had terrible consequences, in that the actor would have one thread performing behavior based on handling messages from its mailbox, and another thread could call into methods on it introducing the exact concurrency issues that we were trying to avoid in the first place by using actors! Those weren't happy times for me.

Avoid Using this

If there is one thing you should take away from this book, this is it. Never refer to any actor class using the open recursive `this` that is so prevalent in object-oriented programming with Java, Scala, and C++. Nothing good can ever come from it.

Imagine you wanted to register an actor via JMX so that you could keep an eye on its internal state in production. It sounds like a great idea because no tool is going to be able to tell you that information unless you expose it yourself. However, the API for registering an MBean in the JDK involves passing an ObjectName to uniquely identify the instance and the reference to the MBean that you wanted to get data from:

```
val mbeanServer = ManagementFactory.getPlatformMBeanServer
def register(actor: InstrumentedActor): Unit = {
  Try { mbeanServer.registerMBean(actor, actor.objectName) } recover {
    case iaee: InstanceAlreadyExistsException => ???
    case mbre: MBeanRegistrationException => ???
    case ncme: NotCompliantMBeanException => ???
    case roe: RuntimeOperationsException => ???
  }
}
```

See how we need to register the "actor" parameter to the mbeanServer? Now, when you try to merely view the internal data attributes, that's not that big of a deal because it's a read-only operation coming from the mbeanServer's thread. In fairness, that means you aren't concerned with absolute consistency or the possibility of seeing partially-constructed objects in JConsole or whatever other mechanism you're using to consume the JMX MBean. But if you define any operations in your MBean, you could very easily introduce concurrency issues and you're toast.

JMX is a simple example, but it's representative of the whole gamut of Observer pattern implementations you might try to use, especially when interacting with legacy Java code and libraries. They'll want you to register the instance of the class to notify when an event occurs and the method to call inside of them, when you only ever want actor messages to be sent.

Instead, if you catch yourself using this in an actor, always change it to self. Self is a value inside of every Akka actor that is an ActorRef to itself. If you want to perform looping within an actor, send a message to that self ActorRef. This has the additional benefit of allowing your system to inject other messages into the looping so they aren't starved for attention while the actor does its work.

The Companion Object Factory Method

In "The Cameo Pattern" on page 20, I switched how I created the Props for my AccountBalanceResponseHandler actor instance to a factory props() method in its companion object. This may seem like an unnecessary implementation detail or a matter of preference, but it is actually a very big deal. When you create a new Akka actor within the body of another Akka actor (as of Akka 2.2 and Scala 2.10.x), a reference to *this* is captured from the actor in which we created the actor. In the Cameo Pattern example, the AccountBalanceResponseHandler would have a direct reference to the AccountBalanceRetriever actor. This isn't something you will typically notice, but it is something you would never actually want to have happen because you *never* want to expose a *this* reference to another actor: it opens the door to having multiple threads running inside of the actor, which is something you should never allow to happen.

There is a proposal to make the Props API based upon the concept of Spores, which are part of SIP-21 (*http://docs.scala-lang.org/sips/pending/spores.html*) and may be included in an upcoming version of the Scala language. By forcing users of a library to pass information in a Spore, they would have to explicitly capture the state they want to pass to the new Akka actor reference, and a this reference to the one who created it could not leak over.

Roland Kuhn, currently the head of the Akka team, is the person who defined this best practice with some help from Heiko Seeberger, Typesafe's Director of Education. But I also see another benefit to this approach. You are putting the information about how to create the Props reference in one place—otherwise, those details are spread around to every place in your code that is creating instances of this actor.

Note that you could use an apply() method instead of a method named props(). I'm not terribly keen on that idea, however—apply() is a method that should return an instance of the type for which the companion object was defined. In this case, the actual return type is an instance of Props. As a result, I don't think it meets the basic contract of what an apply() should do, and I think a method name that describes what you're actually creating is more appropriate.

Here is an example. Historically, we have grown very comfortable with creating actors like this:

```
case object IncrementCount

class CounterActor(initialCounterValue: Int) extends Actor {
  var counter = initialCounterValue
  def receive = {
    case IncrementCount => counter += 1
  }
}

class ParentOfCounterActor extends Actor {
  val counter = context.actorOf(Props(new CounterActor(0)), "counter-actor")
  def receive = Actor.emptyBehavior
}
```

To avoid this potential issue of closing over this, I recommend you instead instantiate the Props for your new actor like this:

```
object CounterActor {
  case object IncrementCount

  def props(counter: Int): Props = Props(new CounterActor(counter))
}
```

```
class CounterActor(initialCounterValue: Int) extends Actor {
  var counter = initialCounterValue
  def receive = {
    case CounterActor.IncrementCount => counter += 1
  }
}

class ParentOfCounterActor extends Actor {
  val counter = context.actorOf(CounterActor.props(0), "counter-actor")
  def receive = Actor.emptyBehavior
}
```

 Use a companion object `props()` factory method to create the instance of `Props` for an Akka actor so you don't have to worry about closing over a reference to `this` from the actor that is creating the new actor instance.

Never Use Direct References

With the exception of using `TestActorRef` (in Akka's TestKit implementation) and getting the `underlyingActor` for unit testing purposes, you should never know the type of an actor. You should only ever refer to it as an `ActorRef`, which will only expose an API of message sending. If you find code that has a reference to an actor by its actual type, you're making it very easy for someone to introduce the exact concurrency issues we talked about in the previous section.

Don't Close Over Variables

This is really a good rule for lambdas in general. Any time you have a lambda, it becomes a closure when you reference state external to that lambda's own scope. And that is okay, so long as the external state you are referencing is immutable. In Java8's upcoming lambdas, they were smart enough to enforce that all closed-over external state must be final, much like it had to be when creating a nested inner class, or anonymous inner class implementation. However, with Java, merely making a field final doesn't mean it is immutable, as we've all come to know (and much to our chagrin).

However, we often take it for granted in actor development that we can use mutable state within an actor without worrying about concurrency because we will only ever have one thread operating inside of it. However, if you close over that mutable state, especially in a deferred operation like a future, you have no idea what the value of that mutable state will be when that deferred operation is actually executed. This was painfully apparent in the sender issue displayed in "The Extra Pattern" on page 9:

```
// BAD!
class MyActor extends Actor {
  var counter = 0;
  def receive = {
    case DoSomethingAsynchronous =>
      counter += 1

      import context.dispatcher
      Future {
        if (counter < 10) println("Single digits!")
        else println("Larger than single digits!")
      }
  }
}
```

This is scary code. We have a counter value that can change with every message that is received. We then defer printing out some information based on the value of that counter. We can't say with any degree of certainty when that future will be executed, as it's dependent not only on whether there are threads available in the Actor's own dispatcher, but also on when the kernel will schedule the thread to a physical core! You will get very indeterministic results if you execute code like this.

If, for whatever reason, you must close over mutable state in a future lambda, immediately copy it into an immutable local field. This will give you assurance that you've stabilized the value locally within the lambdas context to ensure that nothing unexpected can happen to you:

```
// GOOD!
class MyActor extends Actor {
  var counter = 0;
  def receive = {
    case DoSomethingAsynchronous =>
      counter += 1

      import context.dispatcher
      val localCounter = counter
      Future {
        if (localCounter < 10) println("Single digits!")
        else println("Larger than single digits!")
      }
  }
}
```

In this second example, we capture the counter value at the time the message was handled and can be assured that we will have that exact value when the future's deferred operation is executed.

Use Immutable Messages with Immutable Data

Another possible issue is sending data between actors. We all know that while you may define an immutable value, that does not mean that the attributes of that object are immutable as well. Java collections have long been the prime example of this: merely defining their variables as final means that you can't perform reassignment of that variable name to a new instance of the collection, not that the contents of that collection itself can't be changed.

If you find yourself in a position where you need to send a mutable variable in a message to another actor, first copy it into an immutable field. The reasons for this are the same as stabilizing a variable before using it in a future—you don't know when the other actor will actually handle the message or what the value of the variable will be at that time. The same goes for when you want to send an immutable value that contains mutable attributes.

Erlang does this for you with copy on write (COW) semantics, but we don't get that for free in the JVM. Assuming your application has the heap space, take advantage of it. Hopefully, these copies will be short-lived allocations that never leave the Eden space of your garbage collection generations, and the penalty for having duplicated the value will be minimal.

Help Yourself in Production

Asynchronous programming, regardless of the paradigm, is very difficult to debug. Anyone who tells you otherwise is pulling your leg, being sarcastic, or trying to sell you something. If you've merely used a `ThreadPoolExecutor` in Java and spawned runnables, or more recently, tried the `ForkJoinPool`, what happens if something goes awry on the thread that was spawned? Was the thread that sent that other thread off and running notified? No. Unless you made some effort to at least log when errors occur in that other thread, you may never know that the failure even occurred, if you didn't create the `ForkJoinPool` with the constructor that allowed you to register a generic `Thread.Un caughtExceptionHandler` callback.

This is one of the primary reasons that supervisor hierarchies and actors are such powerful tools. Now, we can not only know when failure happens in asynchronous tasks, but we can also define behaviors appropriate to those failures. The same goes for Scala's future implementation, where you can define behavior that is executed asynchronously depending on whether that deferred operation succeeded or failed.

That said, it is up to you, the developer, to come up with ways to give yourself clues about what went wrong in production. We can't merely attach a remote debugging session to the JVM running the bad code because we would have had to start the JVM with the -Xdebug flag set, which would have prevented a lot of very important runtime optimizations in the Just In Time (JIT) compiler from being performed. That would be terrible for our application's performance. So what can we do? Monitor everything!

Make Debugging Easier

First of all, you need to give yourself as much visibility as possible. You want to be able to use tools that will show you what is happening live in production at any time. That means you need to instrument your application with JMX or do something so that you can see the state inside of your actors at runtime. The Typesafe Console is a wonderful tool that will show you all kinds of information based on nonfunctional requirements about your application, but it will not show you internal state. And no tool that I know of will. Whatever you must do, you must make state accessible in production.

Add Metrics

One of the best things you can do is use metrics inside of your application to provide insight as to how well it is performing. I highly recommend you consider using Coda Hale's Metrics library (*http://metrics.codahale.com/*). However, you have to think about what you want to capture before you can add them, such as possibly writing your own Akka actor mailbox to capture information about how quickly messages are handled. Nonetheless, using tools like metrics in your application is extremely helpful, especially when you want to make internal state externally visible, which cannot be provided by profiling tools such as the Typesafe Console.

Externalize Business Logic

One thing that we've learned in object-oriented programming is that encapsulation is key. And generally speaking, I agree. However, before Akka's TestKit came along, the only way to write functional logic that could be tested in isolation (without firing up actors and sending messages that could result in side effects) was to write all business logic in external function libraries.

This has a few added benefits. First of all, not only can we write useful unit tests, but we can also get meaningful stack traces that say the name of where the failure occurred in the function (but only if we define them as `def` methods, not as `val` functions, due to the way Scala's Scope works). It also prevents us from closing over external state, since everything must be passed as an operand to it. Plus, we can build libraries of reusable functions that reduce code duplication.

Since the introduction of Akka TestKit, this is no longer a rule to me. However, I still find it prudent and useful to follow this best practice.

Use Semantically Useful Logging

Let's be honest, it's a pain to write log output. Sometimes we aren't consistent with the logging levels across all developers on a team. And each call to the logger, regardless of whether or not the logging actually occurs, can hurt performance in the aggregate. However, with asynchronous execution of your logic, it is your best tool to figuring out what is happening inside of your application. I've yet to see a tool that replaces it for me.

That said, merely logging isn't enough. We take it for granted that Scala's case classes will provide us with a useful `toString` method, and it certainly beats having to write our own. However, how many times have you looked through such output, with your head going side to side like you're watching a tennis match, looking for just one value inside of some long output string, like that of a collection?

Pretty printing will help you immensely. Be profligate in your logging, but note that Akka's own logging does not have a trace level. At the debug level, include output that will print out in a useful way so that you can quickly look at the output and discern the important field and value, using tabs and carriage returns. For example:

```
// Using the new Scala 2.10 String Interpolation feature here
if (log.isDebugEnabled)
  log.debug(s"Account values:\n\t" +
            s"Checking: $checkingBalances\n\t" +
            s"Savings: $savingsBalances\n\tMoneyMarket: $mmBalances")
```

The reason we check to see if the debug log level is enabled first is so that we don't go through the expense of assembling the output string if we're not actually going to write the statement.

So how do you enable logging in Akka? First of all, set up your configuration file (*application.conf* if this is for your application; *library.conf* if this is for a library JAR) with the following:

```
# I'm using flat config for space considerations, but anyone familiar
# with the Typesafe Config library should understand what I'm doing here
akka.loglevel = "DEBUG"
akka.event-handlers = ["akka.event.slf4j.Slf4jEventHandler"]
akka.actor.debug.autoreceive = on
akka.actor.debug.lifecycle = on
akka.actor.debug.receive = on
akka.actor.debug.event-stream = on
```

An example of the *logback.xml* file could be like so:

```
<?xml version="1.0" encoding="UTF-8" ?>
<configuration scan="true" scanPeriod="5 seconds">
  <appender name="STDOUT" class="ch.qos.logback.core.ConsoleAppender">
    <encoder>
      <pattern>
```

```xml
          %date{ISO8601} %-5level %logger{36} %X{sourceThread} - %msg%n
      </pattern>
    </encoder>
  </appender>

  <appender name="FILE" class="ch.qos.logback.core.rolling.RollingFileAppender">
    <file>effective_akka.log</file>

    <rollingPolicy class="ch.qos.logback.core.rolling.FixedWindowRollingPolicy">
      <fileNamePattern>/tmp/tests.%i.log</fileNamePattern>
      <minIndex>1</minIndex>
      <maxIndex>10</maxIndex>
    </rollingPolicy>

      <triggeringPolicy class="ch.qos.logback.core.rolling.SizeBasedTrigger-
ingPolicy">
      <maxFileSize>500MB</maxFileSize>
      </triggeringPolicy>
      <encoder>
      <pattern>
        %date{ISO8601} %-5level %logger{36} %X{sourceThread} - %msg%n
      </pattern>
      </encoder>
      </appender>

      <logger name = "akka.actor" level = "DEBUG" >
      <appender-ref ref = "FILE" />
      <appender-ref ref = "STDOUT" />
      </logger>

      <root>
              <level value="INFO" />
              <appender-ref ref="STDOUT" />
      </root>
  </configuration>
```

Just put these two files in your classpath (i.e., *src/main/resources* folder). Now you have access to all of the output possible from Akka itself, without having to result to logging each message receive and actor lifecycle event yourself.

Aggregate Your Logs with a Tool Like Flume

If you have a distributed actor application across multiple nodes, you want to use a tool like Flume to aggregate all of your actor logs together. Akka logging is asynchronous and therefore nondeterministic: it's entirely possible that the ordering of the aggregated log output will not be exactly right, but that's okay. Having one rolling log file as opposed to having to look at them across multiple machines is a much simpler task. Just imagine the timestamp variance possibilities if you don't aggregate.

Use Unique IDs for Messages

This is a critical tool for debugging. Every one of your messages should be a case class instance with an ID associated with it. As a general rule, do not pass literals and do not pass objects (though I've always felt it's okay when you pass a case object Start).

Why do I want to do this? Because it makes debugging via log files that much easier. Now, if I know the specific message ID that led to a problem, I can grep/ack/ag (ag is the command of The Silver Searcher) the output logs for all messages containing that ID and view the flow of that message through my system. That is, assuming I logged the output when the message was received and handled.

I've seen implementations where every actor message was passed with a UUID to uniquely identify it. That is great, since the odds of two UUIDs ever being exactly the same is infinitesimal. However, java.util.UUID instances are expensive to create, so unless you're generating billions of messages daily, this may be more unique than you actually need.

For example, would it suffice to use some value where the likelihood of a collision over a day or a few hours was low? We generally know when an error occurs, as far as the timestamp we should expect to see associated with that ID. If we grep the logs, and it returns a bunch of output for when the error occurred, as well as some from the day before or several hours after, we've at least whittled down the output to something manageable, and the ID has been useful. And hopefully cheaper to create. There are GUID generation libraries available with a simple search of the Internet, if you are so inclined.

Tune Akka Applications with the Typesafe Console

One of the biggest questions I encounter among users of Akka is how to use dispatchers to create failure zones and prevent failure in one part of the application from affecting another. This is sometimes called the Bulkhead Pattern. And once I create the failure zones, how do I size the thread pools so that we get the best performance from the least amount of system resources used? The truth is, every application is different, and you must build your system and measure its performance under load to tune it effectively. But here are some tips and tricks.

Note that the Typesafe Console is available for free to all developers and will be integrated into the Typesafe Activator (*http://typesafe.com/activator*) to make it easier to set up and use quickly.

Fixing Starvation

Most people building an Akka application start out with a single ActorSystem, using the default dispatcher settings with a minumum number of threads of 8 and a maximum

---

number of threads of 64. As the application grows, they notice that futures time out more frequently, since futures in Akka actors often use the actor's dispatcher as their ExecutionContext implicitly. Eventually, as more functionality is assigned to be run on threads, the default dispatcher begins to become overloaded, trying to service too many simultaneous tasks.

How do you fix it?

Because of the limited resources of one thread pool for all actors and futures in their application, resource starvation is occurring. When that happens, I recommend that you identify actors using futures and consider where you can use a separate dispatcher or ExecutionContext for those futures so that they do not impact actors with their thread usage. We want to limit the impact of the work of those futures on the actors handling messages in their mailbox. If you have the Typesafe Console, you can see the starvation occuring as the maximum latency in handling messages at the dispatcher level increases.

Does PinnedDispatcher help?

As a temporary workaround, I have noticed some people try to use a PinnedDispatcher for each actor so that starvation is less likely. Actors created with PinnedDispatcher will receive their own dedicated thread that lives up until the keep-alive-time configuration parameter of the ThreadPoolExecutor (default of 60 seconds) is not exceeded. However, this is really not a viable solution for production except for very specific use cases, such as service-oriented actors handling a lot of load. For most other tasks, you want to share resources among actors with similar roles and risk profiles so that you aren't using large amounts of resources dedicated to each actor. In addition, starting and restarting threads takes time, and each has a default size of 512 KB. You will use up your memory very quickly in a system that relies primarily on actors created with PinnedDispatcher.

Failure zones

The key to separating actors into failure zones is to identify their risk profile. Is a task particularly dangerous, such as network IO? Is it a task that requires blocking, such as database access? In those cases, you want to isolate those actors and their threads from those doing work that is less dangerous. If something happens to a thread that results in it completely dying and not being available from the pool, isolation is your only protection so that unrelated actors aren't affected by the diminishment of resources. With the Typesafe Console, you can visualize the performance of your dispatchers so that you can be certain that you have properly provided "bulkheads" between actors doing blocking work and those that should not be affected.

Routers

You also may want to identify areas of heavy computation through profiling, and break those tasks out using tools such as routers. For those tasks that you assign to routers, you might also want them to operate on their own dispatcher so that the intense computation tasks do not starve other actors waiting for a thread to perform their work. With the Typesafe Console, you can visualize the isolation of work via actors and their dispatcher to be certain that the routers are effectively handling the workload.

Sizing Dispatchers

Now the question becomes how to size your dispatchers, and this is where the Typesafe Console can be very handy. In systems where you have several or many dispatchers, keep in mind that the number of threads that can be run at any time on a box is a function of how many cores it has available. In the case of Intel boxes, where hyperthreading is available, you could think in terms of double the number of cores if you know that your application is less CPU-bound. I recommend sizing your thread pools close to the number of cores on the box where you plan to deploy your system and then running your system under a reasonable load and profile with the Typesafe Console. You can then externally configure the thread pool sizes and check the impact at runtime.

The Parallelism-Factor Setting

When using the Typesafe Console, watch the dispatcher's view to see if the latency of message handling is within acceptable tolerances of your nonfunctional requirements, and if not, try adjusting the number of threads required upward. Remember, you're setting the minimum number of threads, the maximum number of threads, and the *parallelism-factor*. This is the ceiling of the number of cores on your box multiplied by that factor is calculated to determine the thread pool size, bounded by the max and min settings you give.

Actor Mailbox Size

The Typesafe Console also shows you something else that is very important to watch— the size of each actor's mailbox. If you see an actor whose mailbox is perpetually increasing in size, you need to retune the threads for its dispatcher or parallelize its task by making it a router so that it has the resources it needs to keep up with the demands placed on it by the system. The receipt of messages into an actor's mailbox can be bursty in nature, but you shouldn't have actors with mailboxes that aren't handling the traffic coming to them fast enough to keep up with the load.

Once you have an idea of the number of threads you need to handle burstiness in your application (if any), sit down with your team and determine the minimum and maximum bounds of each thread pool. Don't be afraid to add a few extra threads to the max to account for possible thread death in production, but don't go overboard.

Throughput Setting

Also, pay close attention to your *throughput* setting on your dispatcher. This defines thread distribution "fairness" in your dispatcher, telling the actors how many messages to handle in their mailboxes before relinquishing the thread so that other actors do not starve. However, a context switch in CPU caches is likely each time actors are assigned threads, and warmed caches are one of your biggest friends for high performance. It may behoove you to be less fair so that you can handle quite a few messages consecutively before releasing it.

Edge Cases

There are a few edge cases. If you have a case where the number of threads is equal to the number of actors using the dispatcher, set the number extremely high, like 1,000. If your actors perform tasks that will take some time to complete, and you need fairness to avoid starvation of other actors sharing the pool, set the throughput to 1. For general usage, start with the default value of 5 and tune this value for each dispatcher so that you get reasonable performance characteristics without the risk of making actors wait too long to handle messages in their mailboxes.

About the Author

Jamie Allen is the director of consulting for Typesafe, the company that makes the Scala programming language, the Akka toolkit, and Play Framework. Jamie has been building actor-based systems with Scala since 2009. Jamie lives in the San Francisco Bay Area with his wife, Yeon, and their three children.

Colophon

The animal on the cover of *Effective Akka* is the black grouse (*Tetrao tetrix*).

The cover image is from Meyers Kleines Lexicon. The cover font is Adobe ITC Garamond. The text font is Adobe Minion Pro; the heading font is Adobe Myriad Condensed; and the code font is Dalton Maag's Ubuntu Mono.

Get even more for your money.

Join the O'Reilly Community, and register the O'Reilly books you own. It's free, and you'll get:

- $4.99 ebook upgrade offer
- 40% upgrade offer on O'Reilly print books
- Membership discounts on books and events
- Free lifetime updates to ebooks and videos
- Multiple ebook formats, DRM FREE
- Participation in the O'Reilly community
- Newsletters
- Account management
- 100% Satisfaction Guarantee

Signing up is easy:

1. Go to: oreilly.com/go/register
2. Create an O'Reilly login.
3. Provide your address.
4. Register your books.

Note: English-language books only

To order books online:

oreilly.com/store

For questions about products or an order:

orders@oreilly.com

To sign up to get topic-specific email announcements and/or news about upcoming books, conferences, special offers, and new technologies:

elists@oreilly.com

For technical questions about book content:

booktech@oreilly.com

To submit new book proposals to our editors:

proposals@oreilly.com

O'Reilly books are available in multiple DRM-free ebook formats. For more information:

oreilly.com/ebooks

Spreading the knowledge of innovators   oreilly.com

CPSIA information can be obtained at www.ICGtesting.com
Printed in the USA
LVOW02s1623050913

351162LV00050B/352/P